THE DENNIS OLSON STORY

Hand to Hand in the Pacific:
THE PERSONAL STORY FROM TARAWA TO GUAM TO OKINAWA

KARL ERIKSEN

iUniverse, Inc.
Bloomington

iUniverse books may be ordered through booksellers or by contacting:

iUniverse
1663 Liberty Drive
Bloomington, IN 47403
www.iuniverse.com
1-800-Authors (1-800-288-4677)

ISBN: 978-1-4502-8298-7 (sc)
ISBN: 978-1-4502-8299-4 (ebook)

Printed in the United States of America

iUniverse rev. date: 03/07/2011

INTRODUCTION

I met Dennis in 2002, at "We Write," a writing group in Grass Valley, California. He was willing to share with me the journals of his experiences as a combat Marine, and agreed also to be interviewed on tape. With this background material I was able to re-create his life in the Marine Corps from boot camp through the battle for Okinawa, also know as "The Last Battle." Our joint collaboration became a project lasting over four years. In the beginning he said, "I'll supply the facts, you write the story." He was never critical of my account, and as the 'color man' in this endeavor I created the dialogue. My initial problem was choosing the proper venue. I started the story as a narrative but soon discovered that to be unwieldy and restrictive. I was advised early on to 'Be Dennis' and write the story that way, which gave me the freedom I needed. The fact that he was willing to share his war experiences was indeed unique. Several of my pre-war buddies had served as combatants in the Marines or in the Army Infantry. None would ever talk of their combat on a personal level. The common retort was, "It's too painful to talk about," or variations there-of. With Dennis it was different. He was willing to share his personal involvement and wanted the absolute horror of it known. He often described his place in the war as being within a ten-foot circle. Nothing beyond that circle involved him but *everything* within it did. What did he mean by that? I'm not exactly sure, but he talked of it several times. When pressed to describe his feelings during battle, he said, "There aren't enough words to adequately explain the fear and terror I felt." Most of the time spent in the war zone, however, was between battles, which had its own brand of misery: Indescribable weather, terrible food, lack of most amenities, and none of the pleasures of life. He was particularly resentful of the treatment the enlisted ranks endured from some of their leaders.

I served during the "big war" in the Navy, spending two years in the South Pacific and in The Philippines, attached to a Carrier Aircraft Service Unit. I lived in the jungle with the mosquitoes, snakes, scorpions, and all the other creatures that creep and crawl, as well as experiencing the weather, which was horrendous. However, the war was won by the *combatants* in the Navy, Marines, the Army, and the Air-Corps who suffered, fought, and died, heroically wresting that otherwise worthless real estate from the Japanese.

I speak from experience when describing the substandard conditions on the rusty old freighters converted to carry troops. I traveled from Guadalcanal to Cebu, The Philippines, on one such vessel, along with the aircraft repair unit I was attached to.

I would apologize for the salty language in this story, but if I did I would also have to apologize for the Marines and the way they were. If anything I underplayed that aspect of their lives, as it was reflective of their reality.

As you will see, Dennis experienced the absolute worst that any war has to offer, and yet miraculously survived

CHAPTER 1

BETIO: THE LANDING

The Marine high command had made a request for more Naval bombardment and aerial bombing of the Betio atoll. It was to be invaded by the Marines the following day, and they wanted to neutralize as much of the Japanese defenses as they could, giving the best chance for success with as minimal a human loss as possible. The Navy had been alternating between bombardment from battleships and cruisers with fourteen, and sixteen-inch guns and aerial bombing with Navy dive bombers. The Navy responded that there was nothing left to bomb. What they didn't know was that the Japanese had prepared for just such a bombardment and invasion when they created that stronghold. Some of the concrete bunkers were several feet thick, and railroad track had been used as reinforcement bar. They were covered with coral, and were invisible. The bombardment and bombing had the effect of simply shifting the coral around. A Japanese general had made the statement: "It will take one million men one hundred years to take this island." In terms of the bombing and bombardment he was correct, as those bunkers could never have been destroyed that way. What he didn't take into account was the tenacity of wave after wave of fighting Marines. My name is Dennis H. Olson. As a private in the United States Marines with the 2nd Division I participated in the invasion of Betio, a Japanese-held atoll in the Tarawa group of the Gilbert Islands. This is my story.

I was running, falling, and crawling in foot-deep water, trying to get onto the beach where I might find some degree of safety. When I was within six or eight feet of shore a very tall Japanese soldier charged toward me with fixed bayonet, shouting, "BANSAI, MOCH-AH-HIII!" He evidently was out of ammunition and intended to kill me with his bayonet.

I was wading and crawling instead of being delivered to the beach by landing craft, because the assault was conducted during slack tide. The boats were running aground on the coral reef eight hundred yards from the beach and could go no farther. It seems someone had failed to take into account the ebb and flow of the tide. Even considering the weird tides at the equator, those boats shouldn't have been sent in unless or until they could float, it seemed to me.

Getting from the troopship to the landing boats was arduous and dangerous. When the order came to, "Saddle up and load the boats by assigned numbers," a cargo net was dropped over the side, and while burdened with full battle gear weighing sixty pounds, we started down. Although there wasn't a heavy sea at the time, the ocean swells made it difficult to transfer from the net to the Higgins boat. A swell could bring the boat up to you, and just as you were about to go for it, drop away and leave you stranded ten feet up waiting for the next swell, hoping your timing would be better. If you had already committed you would have a long fall to the boat. If you didn't fall into the boat the only other place to go was between it and the ship, where you almost certainly would be crushed. That almost happened to me. Just as the Higgins boat reached the top of a surge I jumped. At that instant the small boat swung out and dropped down, and I missed my target. In frantic desperation I was able to grab and hang onto the gunnels, and was pulled in by two alert buddies just before the boat slammed into the ship. The Marine next to me jumped at the same time I did but lacked the dexterity or good luck to grab the gunnels and wasn't seen again. My buddy, Reznik, jumped from the cargo net at the instant the boat dropped away, creating a ten-foot fall, landing on three guys, nearly making casualties of them all.

As the boat shoved off with its load of sixty Marines, several of them looked over the side to see if there was any trace of the guy who didn't make it.

"Keep your goddamn heads down!" Lieutenant Jacobs shouted. "There's nothing we can do about Smitty."

Lieutenant Jacobs had been the platoon leader for just two weeks and the troops weren't sure he was qualified to lead them. He was a recent officers' candidate school graduate; another "ninety-day-wonder".

The men had confidence in the platoon sergeant, who had survived the battle of Guadalcanal. Sergeant Corona got drunk whenever booze was available, and he seemed to find it, or a reasonable substitute, most of the time. On duty however, he was all business, drunk or sober. A hard-nosed, gung-ho Marine.

I popped my head up to see why it was taking so long to reach shore. We appeared to be heading out to sea.

"We're going the wrong way, sir!" I shouted to the lieutenant.

"I told you to keep your goddamn head down!" He shouted again. "We're circling 'till the rest of the boats get loaded, and in formation. You'll get there soon enough."

The cox'n was soon given the signal, gave the engine full throttle, and we were on our way. As we approached to about one thousand yards of the beach we heard a loud rattle on the bow.

Sergeant Corona shouted, "That's heavy machine gun fire coming from shore. When we drop the ramp, haul ass fast."

"Christ!" Reznik shouted. "The bastards are shooting at us. I didn't think there would be anyone left alive after the bombardment."

All the guys started babbling nervously to keep up their courage. We thought it was going to be a soft landing. It didn't make sense. How could there be anyone still alive after three days of bombardment? We had been trained to do combat with a hostile enemy, but when the bullets started flying we were confused and scared.

"At ease!" Corona shouted above the chatter. "Check your piece; make sure you have a clip in secure and a round in the chamber. Keep it on 'safe' until you get off the boat. This may not be a soft touch. Get ready to kill the bastards. We'll assemble on the beach. Good luck."

Just then the boat came to a scraping, grinding stop as it became high-centered on the coral reef. Our landing craft was hopelessly grounded, and along with the machine gun fire we were also receiving heavy artillery rounds, evidenced by loud explosions and water spouts. Sergeant Corona ordered the ramp dropped as the Japs were getting our range. Lieutenant Jacobs didn't agree as we were still too far out. He popped his head up to take a look and fell back dead from a round to his face. Sergeant Corona's order stood and the ramp was dropped. The Marines begin pouring out onto the coral reef and to their deaths. Some were being killed while still on the boat. Sergeant Corona was among the first of those killed as he was at the front when the ramp dropped. Reznik and I jumped over dead bodies and ran forward. I made the decision to go over the side of the ramp instead of straight ahead, for two reasons: I couldn't get around all the dead guys on the ramp, and second, I thought I'd stand a better chance of not being shot if I jumped over the side of the ramp. That was the decision that probably saved my life.

However, instead of stepping into shallow water as expected, I stepped into a bomb crater. The weight of my gear took me to the bottom and held me there. In a panic I jettisoned my helmet, knapsack, haversack, ammunition bandoleer, and hand grenades. Only then was I able to struggle to the surface, gulping air and coughing salt water. I paddled away from the crater to waist-deep water and found myself in the midst of a fierce barrage of heavy machine gun fire.

My thoughts ran from thankfulness for not drowning to the realization that I wasn't going to live through all of that fire.

Hell, I might just as well have stayed in the crater, I'm not going to live anyway. How come none of these bullets are hitting me? Probably if I stand here long enough they will. Maybe I should move out. Which way should I go? Well, of course, toward the beach, dummy. What the hell for? What can I do there? I'm still carrying my carbine but what good is it going to be against all this fire? I should have left it in the crater with all that other crap.

All those thoughts were running through my mind as I was brought back to reality by the sound of the diesel engine from the Higgins boat just vacated. The cox'n was able to free it from the coral by reason of its lightened load, and as it backed off the coral and turned away from the harbor, received a direct artillery hit, fell apart and sank.

I was being shot at not only from the bunkers on shore but from a beached, bombed out hulk of a ship where the Japanese had placed several fifty caliber machine guns. They were successful in directing a deadly crossfire and together with the artillery were annihilating our forces.

Can anyone get to that beach? I don't think so. How can we possibly get there? There's no way. Christ, Marines are being killed all around me, bodies are floating everywhere. I wish I had my helmet because of all the .50 caliber fire. Maybe if I duck under, the bullets will ricochet off the water and not hit me.

Underwater the full impact of the concussion of the artillery shells was gut wrenching, forcing me to abandon that self-protective tactic. Trying to run in the water on the uneven, jagged coral was impossible. The faster I tried to move the more I stumbled and fell. The whole thing just seemed futile, and I felt completely helpless. It reminded me of a dream I once had of being chased but unable to move, seemingly frozen in place. I had no idea the landing could possibly be this bad. It was just the most horrible situation I could ever have imagined. I remember thinking I would be better off if I got hit so it would be over because I knew I wouldn't make it to the beach. There was just no goddamn way I was going to live through that firepower, and I wondered how it would feel to die. I wondered if it would be painful and supposed I would find out in a minute, or maybe a second. I kept slogging along, fully expecting each step to be my last. I saw a long pier off to my left with other guys near the pilings. Are they Japs or Marines? I remember thinking: *They must be Marines.*

Can I make it there? Goddamn I'm scared. I've never been this scared. I hope I can make it to that pier. If I can just get that far I'll find protection behind the pilings. That'll be better than in the open like this. It's a long way; I don't think I can do it. Keep going, Dennis, you might make it. Damn, it's hard to walk in this water. It's like someone is holding me back. I'm almost there. Damn I'm tired, and my legs ache. Just two more steps. There, that does it. I'm safe behind the pilings and I'm still alive. I didn't think I would get this far, but here I am. I'm safe now.

There were several Marines huddled together behind the pilings. I didn't see a familiar face as none were from my platoon, but it felt good to be together with someone. *Maybe I'll get through this after all; I'm not ready to give up yet.*

Those guys were in bad shape: three dead and six badly wounded. They would all be gone if they didn't move out soon. If I was going to get to the beach and do any good when I got there I needed to gather up some equipment from the dead guys. I got a helmet from the only guy who hadn't received shots to his head, and a bandoleer of ammunition and hand grenades from another. One in the group was a flame thrower operator. I wondered how he had gotten that far, burdened with that heavy piece of equipment. I admired his commitment. I'm pretty sure I would have dumped it.

"What do you think we oughta' do, Mac?" He asked.

"Hell, I don't know no more than you, except I know we can't stay here."

"Here they come," shouted the flame thrower man, pointing to a line of waterspouts heading straight toward us.

We all scrambled behind the pilings, grateful for the protection as the machine gun rounds begin hitting all around us and into the pilings. Artillery shells started exploding nearby.

"They're zeroing in on us," another guy shouted. "Let's get the hell out of here."

"How about the wounded?" Someone else asked.

"Drag 'em along. Maybe we'll find a corpsman on the beach," I said. "if the dead guys have grenades, bring them too; we might get a chance to throw 'em at those guys shooting at us; give 'em a little taste of this shit they're feeding us."

We struck out toward shore from piling to piling, receiving heavy fire. The guy I was dragging died so I let him go, but continued on from one piling to the next. I glanced around to see how the others were doing, but the only one still with me was the guy carrying the flame thrower; all the others were gone. Then he got hit. He left one piling and headed for the one I was behind. I heard the fifty caliber shells hitting the equipment he was carrying, ping, ping, ping. Then he screamed as he caught one and went down.

The water was knee deep so I tried crawling, thinking I'd make a smaller target. I crawled to about fifteen feet from shore, where I ran into an obstacle. The Japanese had strung barbed wire between five-foot-tall concrete pyramids spaced about ten feet apart. I got tangled up in wire but was able to work my way to one of the pyramids, using it for cover while I freed myself.

While doing that I was receiving rounds from two different directions, forcing me to duck from one side to the other as incoming waterspouts indicated the direction of the fire. I knew they would get me soon if I didn't move out, and since the water was only about a foot deep, decided to make a run for shore.

Suddenly a very tall Japanese Marine came charging at me with fixed bayonet. I was almost too stunned to react.

"Bansai! Mock-ah-hiiii!" He screamed.

We had been told about the Japanese Special Naval Landing Force. They were described as the elite, the best. They were the Samurai!

What the hell is he doing out here? Why the bayonet? Why doesn't he shoot? He must be out of ammunition, or maybe wants the satisfaction of hand-to-hand killing.

I lurched to my right to avoid the bayonet thrust and tripped over a coconut log, falling sideways causing the blade to miss by inches. His momentum carried him about six feet beyond me, and in that life-saving instant I was able to roll onto my side and level my carbine in his direction. As he turned to make another attack I pulled the trigger, wondering if my carbine would fire as designed or blow up in my face. The barrel was probably full of water. The first bullet tore into his chest, stopping him in his tracks. He screamed and momentarily stood motionless, face distorted by a look of surprise and agony. As he fell toward me I kept squeezing the trigger, pouring more slugs into him at point-blank range. Slowly he caved in, screaming as he fell dead.

He ended up about ten inches from me. There we lay, face to face, mere inches apart. His eyes were staring in disbelief, mouth wide open, screaming without sound. His head was in about six inches of water, and the lapping waves rotated it back and forth as if he were saying, "No, no, no."

I stared at him and was surprised to hear myself scream, "I got ya, ya sonofabitch." Then was further surprised to hear myself mumble, "Sorry."

A strange thing happened after the momentary exhilaration of realizing I had been victorious in that battle. I had a feeling of sorrow for having killed him. I had never killed before and was overwhelmed with mixed emotions of panic, fear, and remorse. I felt awful thinking about his family and how they would feel.

Now I knew it hurt to get killed, or why would he scream like that? Maybe he wanted to die like a Samurai. I couldn't help thinking, had the situation been reversed I would have had a bayonet thrust into some part of my body and my death would certainly have been more painful than the quick death from a lot of bullets. As all these thoughts raced through my head I realized I was being shot at.

I scrambled about twenty yards up the beach to a five-foot-high coconut log sea wall. In a crouched position I ran parallel to the wall, which curved along the perimeter of the beach, putting me beyond view and range of the machine guns on the dreaded, beached ship. I joined some other survivors and hunkered down against the log wall in relative safety.

Suddenly I realized how tired I was. I was safe for the moment but knew sooner or later I would have to go over the wall and meet the enemy. A few had already tried but were killed as soon as they put their heads up. As I leaned back and looked out into the bay I saw bodies strewn about on the beach and floating in the water. The tide was coming in and the Japanese marine I killed was starting to float off the beach, mingling together with dead Marines. Soon there would be no beach and I would have to move out. I wondered what was on the other side of the wall. Hell, I knew what was on the other side!

"Anybody got a dry cigarette?" I asked as I hunkered down against the log wall.

No one answered.

If I never move from this spot that'll be OK with me. I've never been this exhausted. I had no idea anything could be this dreadful. No amount of training could have prepared me for this nightmare.

My dad told me about the First World War, when he was with the Fourth Marine Division at Belleau Wood. They left the trenches and charged into the enemy lines and the machine gun fire of the Germans. They were tangled in barbed wire and almost nobody lived through the charge. My dad said he was glad when he got shot. Being wounded ended the war for him.

This is the same damn thing. Why don't the Navy guns open up on those fifty calibers in the burned-out ship? It's hard to see how anyone can live through this cross fire. How come they sent us in at low tide?

Landing boats were still coming in, and so was the tide, which allowed the boats to get closer in before running aground. They were receiving the same fierce machine gun and artillery fire we had, but for not as long a time. The curve in the beach protected them from the guns on the grounded ship as they got closer in, and the artillery shells were going over their heads.

Some of the tanks and Amtrak's were getting to the beach, and a lot of the guys were following them in, but they could go no farther because of the coconut-log seawall. An officer with a field phone reached shore and sent the coordinates of the beached ship to the Navy and a fourteen-inch shell from a cruiser ended their rein of terror.

The log seawall that had provided protection to all of us lucky enough to reach the shore was preventing the amtraks and tanks from moving beyond the beach to confront the enemy. They climbed up, than tumbled back as their underside was hit by Japanese artillery. The officer with the field phone called for the Navy to blast an opening in the seawall with their big guns.

Several Marines were making their way toward that area, unaware of the plan. Those on shore were frantically yelling and trying to wave them away but unfortunately failed. The guys trying to reach the beach saw the wall as their savior, but the destruction of the wall was soon to be theirs as well. I saw black puffs from the guns on a cruiser, heard the shrill sound of shells flying through the air, then the explosion as they hit their target. It was like a slow-motion scene in a movie as I watched bodies and body parts fly into the air then come down, some in the water, others on the beach. Twenty yards of the seawall was destroyed, enabling the rest of us to advance on the enemy.

While waiting for orders to advance I heard someone yell out my name. "Hey Olson, over here! I got a letter for you."

I hardly recognized Corporal Johnson, the company clerk, as he crawled closer and handed me the letter. Johnson was a spit-and-polish, ear-banging, do-it-by-the-book, baby-faced little guy who always avoided shit details. I was surprised he hadn't found a way to stay clear of this situation. A bullet had creased his cheek and he looked worse than many of the others, soaked in blood, seemingly unaware of his condition.

"Dude, you need to search out a corpsman and get patched up. You look like shit."

"Yeah I know, Olson. I got mail for some of our guys and I gotta deliver it to them first. Have you seen Smitty?"

"Yeah, I have, Johnson, but you're gonna have to send that letter to the Dead Letter Office. He got smashed between the ship and our landing craft. You need to find a corpsman pronto and get yourself taken care of. I doubt if any of those guys you're carrying mail for are still alive."

"Thanks, Olson," he said as he headed down the beach clutching a handful of letters.

The letter he so gallantly delivered to me was from the Internal Revenue Service admonishing me for not filing a 1942 Income Tax Return.

CHAPTER 2
THE BATTLE

Another officer arrived and gave orders to the fragments of several platoons to assemble into combat units and follow the tanks through the breach. "Fan out and take cover as soon as you get beyond the wall. Pass the word."

The first tank through the breach was hit by an artillery shell, lost a track and flipped over on its side. Another received a direct hit but the next two made it through. I was waiting for one to follow that I thought would make it but the lieutenant was running up and down the beach prodding the jarheads to get off their asses and join the war. I decided I couldn't hold out any longer. I, and some others, jumped in behind the next tank going over the hump. It linked up with three other tanks and together was able to make a mass attack. We ran forward crouched behind our iron monster of choice, which was drawing a fierce barrage of artillery rounds. A marine near me received a direct hit from a Japanese artillery shell meant for the tank we were following. We were showered with blood, body parts and flesh, which we were unable to remove for four days. One instant he was there, then he wasn't. He just disappeared. The tank to my right took a direct hit and seconds later the one I was following was also hit. Some of the guys dove into a huge bomb crater, so I joined them, and not an instant too soon. Six or seven others nearby were raked with machine gun fire, knocking them down like ten-pins.

As the tanks were destroyed, so were the Marines following them. Another tank came grinding through the gap, followed by more Marines. They were in enemy territory, receiving a fierce barrage of heavy machine gun, and artillery fire, as well as exploding mortar shells. The shouts of officers, and the screams of wounded men added to that dreadful cacophony. Forward movement faltered as the lethal deluge slashed through our ranks.

I was in the crater together with six others, all grateful for the protection it afforded us. Corporal Bost was the oldest at about twenty-three and was carrying a Browning Automatic, Rifle. Another introduced himself as Joe Wilson, but said his friends called him Torch. He was carrying a flame thrower and flippantly said, "Anyone got a smoke? I got the lighter."

The rest of us carried carbines and hand grenades. We sat there dazed and confused, waiting for something to happen. After a few minutes I said to Bost, "You've got the stripes so you call the shots. Where do we go from here?"

He seemed disoriented as he mindlessly massaged the stock of his rifle. Though my words seemed to bring him out of it he was resentful at suddenly being put in command of that deadly situation. He was unsure about what we should do. The options were to sit tight and wait for reinforcements or vacate our temporary safety and try to hook up with another outfit. If we stayed in the crater a grenade or mortar could come our way, so the decision was made to vacate and join the war. We were about to move out when a corpsman in bad need of a corpsman tumbled into the hole. He was shot in the arm and in the leg. We took time to patch him up with his medical supplies, help him out of the crater and point him in the direction of the beach.

As we prepared a second time to leave, Bost, looking over the edge, said, "Hold it. We're getting company. I know him. It's John the Bomb."

John crawled over the edge and slid down to join us. He was a ruddy, round-faced giant of a man with eyeglasses pasted to his face with adhesive tape. He carried a carbine and two bandoleers stuffed with blocks of composition C explosives.

"Anybody got a drink of water?" He asked.

"Hell no, we lost our gear getting ashore," Bost answered.

John told us of a bunker about fifteen yards to our right and thought we could take it since we were on its blind side.

"It's worth a try." Bost said. "We'll surround Torch and try to get to the entrance. Take a look, Olson, and see if you think it's time to go."

I clawed my way to the edge, motioned the others to follow and helped pull Torch up. The rest of the guys heaved themselves out and, running in a half crouch, jumping over dead Marines and coconut logs, avoiding debris and dodging bullets, made it to the entrance of the bunker. Lying flat we waited for Torch to pour a stream of fire through the opening. Two Japs tried to run out but were stopped by a white-hot blaze and a volley of rifle fire. As Torch continued the burn, screams of terror and agony came from within. After a brief time to clear the air we cautiously crawled into the bunker, apprehensive about what awaited us. Several of the enemy was still alive, screaming and writhing on the floor. They were quickly quieted with a bullet. Although the extensive training I had received was all about killing, it didn't paint that picture, nor did it teach how to deal with a scene such as that. I forced myself to the reality that they were the enemy who had so recently been delivering the blistering firepower killing so many of my fellow Marines trying to reach the beach. I thought about the Japanese marine I had killed on the beach who had every intention of bayoneting me. Both of us couldn't walk away alive. One had to die, and I figured better him than me.

The stench in that place was almost unbearable because of the acrid fumes from the flame thrower intermixed with the pungent smell of burning uniforms and human flesh. Worst of all was the gagging, fetid odor of excrement, which had been released as the men died.

Torch said, "Let's get the hell out of here; I can't stand the smell"

"Not till I get a drink," John the Bomb said. "I ain't going no further without water."

Corporal Bost took command, ordering everyone to look for canteens, water bottles, or campaign cans. We thought we might get lucky and find some sake. We found several canteens of water on the dead Japs but no sake. One of the guys found a case of new pistols, and I discovered a locked safe. We were all curious to know what was in it. John the Bomb wanted to blow it, saying he might gain experience for a future career, but Corporal Bost was afraid if he packed enough Composition C to crack the safe he would kill us all. John assured us he knew what he was doing and that no one would get hurt. It took about five minutes to pack in the charge and move enough boxes and cases to form a blast shield. From time to time we went to the entrance for a breath of fresh air and to see if everything was clear outside.

We took cover as John set the primer and made a dash for the safe area. The concussion collapsed the blast shield, and we crawled from under the boxes like punch-drunk penguins. What the safe yielded was money, a lot of money; Japanese as well as American. Many bundles of twenty-dollar bills, all with HAWAII stamped across the face. We concluded it was invasion currency and were now faced with the dilemma of what to do with this fortune. We decided to put it in sandbags and bury it in the bunker. We'd come back when the shooting stopped, dig it up, and divide it. Some of the sandbags lining the walls were emptied and refilled with currency. It was a simple matter to dig a hole in the sand floor and bury our loot.

It was time to vacate that stinking hole and re-join the war. As we reached the exit we were met by an officer and six riflemen. He identified himself as Captain Thornton.

"What's inside the bunker?" He asked.

"A bunch of dead Japs, and the Marines who made 'em that way," I answered.

His arm was badly ripped and bleeding from shrapnel, but he seemed not to notice as he directed his attention to Bost.

"Get your group together, corporal. You're gonna be part of my combat team. We're preparing to launch an assault on the power station."

It was a concrete building half under-ground and half above ground with a ten-foot-thick roof and walls. The entrance was in the shape of a T. The leg of the T led to the interior, and access was gained by way of the cross of the T. It had withstood naval bombardment and dive bomber attacks and was going to be taken only the hard way, the Marine way. We were gathered behind a disabled tank making plans for the assault. Captain Thornton wanted three men at each opening of the T to lob in hand grenades, creating a large explosion, making it possible for Torch to enter and direct his flame into the interior.

Corporal Bost said. "Sir, if one grenade goes off before the others it could blow the remaining grenades back on us. We don't want that."

The Captain, seemingly ignoring Bost's comment, was silent for a moment, then said,

"All of you pull the pin but hold your grenade while I count to three, then toss them in together."

The plan worked well and all grenades went off at the same time, creating one huge explosion. Torch, following the plan, moved into position and was able to direct his flame into the interior, along with two Marines with automatic weapons pouring in lead. However, return fire from within brought all of them down and the torch was passed, so to speak, to another Marine, who also was killed. Captain Thornton shouted for everyone to get out as he took command of the flamethrower. He had only enough time to get off a short burn before he also was shot dead.

The rest of us rushed in and in, a frenzy begin shooting every Japanese soldier, dead or alive. Thus did the bunker change ownership.

As we were preparing to vacate the premises a loud booming voice rang out from the entrance, demanding, "who's in charge here?"

"No one," someone answered. "The captain just got killed."

"Listen up. I'm Major Schmidt, and I'm taking charge. Get all the bodies out; lay the dead Marines in a row outside, and toss the Japs into a bomb crater. I'm setting up a command post in here. Get cracking."

It was a gruesome job carrying the burned, mangled bodies out. The stench was indescribable. Bost and I worked together and along with the others did what we were told, dumping the twenty or so Japanese soldiers into a nearby bomb crater. The Marines were laid out, but not too close as they didn't smell any better than the dead Japs. Major Schmidt was organizing a defense of his command post and Bost and I, along with about twenty others, were tagged to be part of it. He designated several locations where he wanted foxholes.

"Team up with a buddy and dig two-man foxholes deep enough to protect against a counterattack. You'll be in your foxhole all night without relief. Stay awake. Your life depends on it. This is an important assignment, and I don't want any fuck-ups. Get cracking."

"Where did John the Bomb go?" Bost asked.

"He hauled ass after Major Schmidt showed up." I answered.

I teamed up with a guy named Link. Billy Joe Link, he said. We "got cracking" and fashioned a two-man hole about six feet long and four feet wide. When we were finished, it was dinnertime and getting dark. I was hungry enough to eat dirt since I hadn't had anything since five o'clock that morning on the troopship. I didn't realize K rations could taste so good, and managed to wolf down a double ration. After dinner I smoked two cigarettes and was beginning to feel normal for the first time that day.

"Where you from, Link?" I asked.

"I'm from Texarkana, Texas; not Texarkana, Arkansas. There's two Texarkana's. I'm from the one in Texas. Did you know there was two Texarkana's?" Not waiting for an answer, he continued, "Most people don't know there's two Texarkana's, did you know there was two Texarkana's, Olson?"

"I didn't know that," I said, adding, "but I do now. How old are you, Link?"

"I'm sixteen."

"Aren't you supposed to be eighteen to join the Marines?"

"Yeah, but I lied, and my daddy signed a paper to get me in because I wanted to be a Marine because my daddy was in the first World War and—"

I interrupted him, saying, "We need to work out a plan to take turns sleeping. I think we need to change off sleeping every hour. Is that OK with you?"

"Yeah, that's OK, Olson. You can sleep first."

My first day of combat was nearly over. I don't know what I expected; certainly not what it was. From thinking we would walk in almost unopposed by reason of the Naval bombing and shelling to the devastating reality of what it was, was a terrible shock. I couldn't get the events of the day out of my mind; all the guys getting killed when the ramp dropped, the dead guys floating in the harbor as I made my way toward the pier, killing the guy trying to kill me. I wished I could go to sleep and forget everything, or better yet, wake up and find out it was just a bad dream. It was a long way from over. I figured I'd better forget about that day and concentrate on the night ahead and what I needed to do to stay alive.

What was learned from the Guadalcanal campaign had become part of our training at Samoa. It taught that Japanese soldiers clad only in a loincloth would silently crawl on their bellies until they were next to a foxhole, then roll in on top of the occupant with knife in hand and kill him.

That's what happened to Billy Joe Link and me. It was my turn to sleep and I was lying on my back holding my field knife with the blade pointing up and the butt end resting on my chest. If a visitor dropped in he would hopefully drop in on my knife.

It was in the wee hours just before dawn when a Japanese soldier hurtled into our foxhole completely over me, landing on top of Billy Joe Link. I struck out in the dark with my knife and connected with what I hoped was our attacker. My knife was stuck in his head and I couldn't get it out. I decided that all I could do was to lie still with these dead guys till it got light and hope I didn't get another visitor.

I wondered if Reznik made it through the day. I remember thinking he probably didn't get off the boat alive as I didn't think many of the guys did. *Maybe I'm the only one,* I thought. I jumped over the side of the ramp because the dead guys were blocking the way. Going over the side was the only way I could get off the boat, and that's what saved my life. I thought Reznik jumped over the side, too. Maybe he jumped in the bomb crater and didn't come up.

When it got lighter I was glad to see my kabar knife wasn't stuck in Link's head but rather was in the head of the Jap soldier. I put my foot against him and pulled my knife out, and saw that he had a knife in each hand and had made a goddamn bloody mess out of Billy Joe Link. I had never seen such a ghastly sight. His face was chopped up beyond recognition.

As bad as the landing was, the foxhole affair somehow seemed worse, because of the personal aspects of it I suppose.

"Just another statistic, Olson," Bost said. "sad as it is, you need to get over it."

I was visibly shaken and he was trying to ease my pain I suppose. I also, correctly, supposed this wasn't to be the last of such experiences I could look forward to, if indeed I lived long enough.

Bost and his partner, a guy they called, Tex, made it through the night, but Lincoln and his foxhole partner were both stabbed to death, and the Jap who jumped them was in the hole with them with a trench knife stuck in his face. All three were in a pool of blood.

We spent the next three days of the battle busy fighting off groups of Japs trying to retake the command post. The fighting intensified, and several Marines had been added to our group, so we were able to hold our position; but we lost several of our guys killed or wounded.

Hillman was in a foxhole a few yards to my left, and during the firefight on the third night got hit but not killed. He called several times for a corpsman but they must have been busy or didn't hear him. I crawled over to see if I could help. I covered him with my poncho so the light from my zippo wouldn't be seen. When I saw the bullet hole in the back of his helmet and blood all over his face I figured he was a goner. I told him to lie back and die quietly to avoid attracting the enemy, then made my way back to my hole.

In the morning he was gone. What the hell could happen to a guy with a bullet in his head? Maybe the Japs slipped in and took his body, or maybe he went to heaven.

"What happened to Hillman?" I asked Bost.

"Beats the shit out of me Olson. Maybe the noise bothered him and he went home."

"You seem to have developed a sense of humor. Are you starting to enjoy the war?"

"Not even. I heard this might be the last day of the fighting. We need to stay alive one more day, Olson, then we got it made in the shade."

Later in the day a group of eight or ten wounded Marines were heading for the beach to be taken to the hospital ship. I couldn't believe what I was seeing. Reznik was among them. His head and shoulder were bandaged and bloody, and he was limping. His left pant leg had been cut away, and he had a bloody bandage wrapped around that leg.

I went to meet him. "You're looking good, dude. Where you been, and what have you been doing? I thought you were dead."

"I thought you was dead too, Olson. I been killing Japs like you wouldn't believe it. They damn near killed me too. How you been, buddy?"

"I'm still alive," I answered. "This has been one bad motherfucker, hasn't it?"

"It's worse than that, buddy. I'll see ya later. I gotta get to that hospital ship; I'm hurting big time."

That was the best news I had since this whole thing started. He looked terrible but seeing him alive gave me a glimmer of hope that things might work out; a small glimmer, but a glimmer never the less.

Another surprise! I couldn't believe what I was seeing; Hillman was heading our way swinging his helmet. He had a large bandage, covering his nose and most of his face.

"Hey, Hillman, over here. How you doing, buddy? I thought you was dead."

"Just a giant headache. I came back to find the rest of my nose. You guys haven't seen it, have you?"

Another comedian; it must be contagious.

"What the hell you talking about? What happened? The last I saw, you was in your foxhole with a bullet in your brain." I said.

"My story is in the helmet. Look here."

He handed me his helmet and showed us the bullet hole, and a big dent in the liner. It seems the bullet scratched his face pretty good and clipped off the end of his nose as it exited his helmet. That was where all the blood came from when I was checking him out and thought he was dying

"That's the damnedest thing I ever seen," Bost said. "you oughta send your helmet to 'Ripley's Believe It Or Not'."

On the fourth day of the battle, Major Schmidt brought us up to date.

"Men, it's almost over. I've been informed the battle is won, and mopping up operations are being conducted throughout the island. But the remaining enemy forces aren't surrendering. They're conducting suicide attacks, and our forces are sustaining heavy losses. However, the Japanese are being annihilated as they prefer death to surrender. The Japanese general who proclaimed one million men couldn't take the island in one hundred years hadn't taken into account the tenacity and fighting skills of the Marines. You all have done honor to the Corps and have upheld the tradition of the best fighting force in the world. Congratulations."

The following day a strange thing happened when the shooting was over. A small detachment of British soldiers appeared, dressed in freshly starched uniforms with knee-length pants. They marched sharply to the tallest palm remaining and proceeded to hoist the Union Jack. That was a total affront to the battle-weary Marines who had just taken that island from the Japanese at tremendous cost. First one marine, then another, then another, took aim at that insulting piece of cloth until it fluttered to the ground. There was no way in hell that any flag other than the Stars and Stripes was going to be raised on that atoll. There we stood, the ragged, the dirty, the wounded, at attention while our flag—that of the United States of America, was raised.

The British detachment made a hasty retreat. We had been told but had forgotten, the Gilbert Islands, which included Tarawa, were a British Protectorate. It seemed to me they had done a piss-poor job of 'protectoring' it.

CHAPTER 3

AFTER THE BATTLE

Later that day Corporal Bost told me I was to be part of a detachment to deliver some surviving Japanese solders to one of the ships at anchor in the harbor.

We marched sixteen or eighteen prisoners to the beach and, since the tide was in, commandeered a Higgins boat on the beach. We assumed we would have no problem following the orders to deliver them to one of the Naval ships at anchor in the harbor. However the Officer of the Deck on the cruiser we stopped at wouldn't allow them on his ship. Bost. directed the cox'n to another warship nearby where we got the same response. No one wanted our prisoners so the cox'n of the Higgins boat solved the problem. He shot them all and dumped them over the side.

The belief system I was raised with in terms of respect for human life had no place there. All the rules had been changed. What's unacceptable and abhorrent within a civilized society was acceptable, even honored out there. To witness and to have been part of those shocking events was hard for me to deal with. I hoped in time I'd find a way. I also hoped that would be the last battle I'd be asked to participate in, but doubted that would be the case.

I, along with other survivors, was assigned to the burying detail. Dead bodies were everywhere I looked, literally thousands. Many had received a clean shot to some part of their body while others had their head blown off or had lost their legs or their arms, or both. I had a hard time looking at that mass of humanity who had so recently been alive and well. Even after all these years I dream of that scene. In my dreams I see bodies floating in the air, mostly they're half bodies, which seems to make it even worse.

The CBs (Construction Battalion) arrived on the island and were unloading their equipment. A top priority for them was to dig a very long ditch six feet deep and the width of a tractor blade for us so we could bury our dead. We worked in teams of two and our job was to remove the dog tags, roll the body onto a blanket and lay it in the ditch side by side with all the others. We gave the dog tags to the sergeant in charge of Graves Registration. A tally of the bodies without a dog tag, because of mutilation, was given to the sergeant so a relatively accurate count could be kept of those killed. I suppose those without dog tags were listed as unknown soldiers. It was an assignment that lasted two days and was more upsetting than I'm able to describe. Having been in that hot tropical sun, they were all in varying states of decay depending on when they were killed. The smell defied description. I fashioned a mask of sorts from a tee shirt, but it didn't help. Formal burial was to take place at a later date, we were told.

The Japanese soldiers were unceremoniously dumped into bomb craters and covered with coral sand.

We took the island from the Japanese in seventy-two hours, but at the tremendous loss of over 3,000 killed or wounded. The Japanese lost 5,000 soldiers.

Reznik and I were the only ones from our boat to get to the beach. The other fifty-eight were killed. I think a lot about the three days following the landing; how close to death I had constantly been; how many killed and wounded. The worst to see and hear were the wounded men and their agonizing screams. I wondered if any of us would ever be able to regain a sense of reality after that nightmare.

Betio is a small atoll, no more than a mile wide and about three miles long. How in the name of God could that worthless rock be worth the lives of eight thousand human beings? I had a hard time justifying that tradeoff even when the strategic reasons were understood.

The CBs were working twenty-four hours a day extending the length of the runway and putting down steel matting. That task was completed in a few days and the Army Air Corps immediately flew in medium-size bombers. The reason we took that island away from the Japs in the first place was so the Japanese-held islands to the north could be bombed from there. It was just another small step in the long journey to Japan, the birthplace of all this death and destruction.

I decided to look up my financial partners and try to retrieve our investment. Corporal Bost, now Sergeant Bost according to the stripes he was wearing, told me he and John the Bomb were the only ones still alive. When we found John his comment, when told of the death of our other partners, was, "Too bad about the others, but what the hell, look on the bright side; we only gotta divide the loot three ways now."

Bost, turning to me, said, "Congratulations on your promotion."

"What promotion?" I asked.

"Didn't you hear? It was posted this morning. If your name is Dennis Olson you're now Corporal Dennis Olson."

I was glad to hear that, if it was true. Corporal is the most comfortable non-com rating as it keeps you off most of the shit details without burdening you with a great deal of responsibility. The sergeants were blessed with that, and as far as I was concerned were welcome to it.

"We can thank Major Schmidt for our promotions," Bost said. "He appreciated the way we kept the Japs out of his command post and off his ass."

"John, what happened to you after we killed all the Japs in the power station and Major Schmidt showed up and took over?" I asked.

"Major Schmidt showed up, that's what happened. Him and me don't get along too good. He was my company commander when we was back on Samoa, and he was a captain then. Anyway, one night I slipped on down to the little village there to get drunk on tubaa and get laid. I brought some tubaa back and gave it to the guys in my hut."

"So what's the big deal about that? I think we all did that," Bost said.

"The big deal about that was them guys that drank it got sick and fucked up so bad they had to fly 'em to a hospital in New Zealand, and the captain found out I was the one that gave 'em the tubaa."

"How come you didn't get sick and all fucked up like they did?" I asked.

"Because I didn't drink the same tubaa they drank. I bought that shit from some gook on the way back to camp, but I was already wiped out so I passed out when I got back and I didn't drink any of it."

"So what happened when they found out you was the one that gave it to 'em?"

"I went before Captain Schmidt and he chewed ass for quite a while and called me a bunch of names and busted me down from corporal to private. I already felt like shit because them guys was my buddies and I damn sure wouldn't have gave 'em that tubaa if I knew it was gonna fuck em up."

"So how come you hauled ass at the power station? He couldn't bust you any lower then you already were."

"It wasn't what *he'd* do to me. It's what *I* might do to him is the reason I hauled ass. I'm still pretty damn pissed about getting busted and listening to all that shit he dumped on me. I think I would have been tempted to put a little Comp C in his mess kit or something like that."

John wanted to proceed with the money recovery project, so we agreed to meet at the burned-out bunker that night. While digging for our treasure, in walked Captain Steele, the new company commander. He congratulated us on working nights filling sand bags, but on closer examination discovered what was in the sand bags. He examined the money and was silent for several moments, probably trying to figure out how best to handle this delicate situation, then said. "Men, I'm going to turn this money over to the CO, and I'm not going to implicate you. The less said about this, the better off you'll be. "I hope you'll see that to be the best solution, though I appreciate how it must feel to lose this fortune."

John the Bomb, ready to make any compromise, said, "Captain, is there any way we can work out a 'share the wealth' program? I for one would be more than happy to share this plentiful bounty, and I'm sure Sergeant Bost and Corporal Olson feel the same way."

Captain Steele, bristling at that suggestion, said, "Private, this is no more a matter of negotiation than any other issue."

Then, taking a more conciliatory attitude, he continued, "This bunker has been under surveillance since we inspected it when the shooting stopped. The fact that the door was blown off the safe caused us to reach the conclusion it had contained something of value, and whatever that was, we wanted it."

That ended our get-rich-quick opportunity. I would have been happy if it had worked out but actually wasn't upset it didn't. My dad was a firm believer in hard work and often said, "If you don't earn it, you don't deserve it," or something like that.

I had been puzzled about a weapon the Japs used against us when we were trying to get to the beach and decided to ask this guy about it.

"Captain, can I ask you a question? It has nothing to do with the money."

"Go ahead, corporal, ask away. Whether I answer depends on the question."

"Sir, when we were attempting to reach the shore there was an artillery piece the Japs were using against us. It was different from anything we have, at least that I'm aware of. It wasn't like load-fire, load-fire, load-fire. It fired constantly, boom, boom, boom, boom. My question is, do you know what kind of a weapon that was?"

"That was a British piece, corporal...what's your name?"

"My name is Olson, sir. Corporal Dennis Olson."

"Corporal Olson. In answer to your question. It was a British piece the Japs captured from them when they surrendered at Singapore. It's quite an interesting weapon. It fires eight-inch shells from two barrels. One barrel fires as the other recoils, then as that barrel recoils, the other fires, creating a constant barrage, as I'm sure all of you can attest to as you so courageously fought your way toward the beach. It was used against the warships standing offshore until the landing, than it became an anti-personnel weapon."

"Thanks for the information, sir."

Bost had a question for the Captain. "If you know the answer, sir, can you tell me why we were sent in at the time of a slack tide, causing our landing craft to high-center on the coral a thousand yards out, instead of waiting for high tide?"

The Captain was quiet for a few moments before answering.

"That question begs an answer, sergeant, but one I'm not qualified to give. It goes to many issues, and I would be stepping beyond my limits if I were to attempt an answer. I speak for myself, however, when I say I'm profoundly sorry for the loss of so many Marines. I wish you all the best of luck, and hope you live through the rest of the war."

So ended our dreams of wealth. I for one was glad Captain Steele hadn't implicated us. John the Bomb felt he had been cheated out of what was rightfully his. I heard the new C.O. was a colonel recently arrived from a desk job in the States. It's hard to know how it would have come out if our part in that caper had been revealed to him. It probably worked out as it should have.

Chapter 4

GARRISON DUTY

Part 1

Tarawa was declared secure, and what was left of the 2nd Division was sent to New Zealand to refill the empty ranks with replacements, and R & R for those who survived Tarawa. That didn't include the 2nd anti-aircraft artillery, AAA Battalion, which I was a member of as a radar operator. We were to remain on garrison duty to protect the island.

Supply ships were arriving in the harbor daily, their cargo was being off-loaded onto barges and brought ashore. The island was a beehive of activity as several military units were in the process of setting up for the part they were to play on the island. The CBs were working around the clock extending the length of the airstrip so the Army Air Corps could bring in their bombers.

The Japs were dropping bombs on us almost every night, and until we got our defenses set up we were vulnerable. Top priority had been given to the assembly and installation of our 740-D Radar and our AAA. Our armament included four 90 millimeter guns, over two dozen 40 mm's and I don't know how many .50 caliber machine guns. Filling hundreds of sandbags for their protection was heavy, butt- busting grunt work. The temperature hovered between one hundred ten and one hundred thirty, depending on cloud cover and rain. The fortifications had been set up so the guns could be used for anti-aircraft as well as anti-personnel. I didn't want to read too much into the anti-personnel thing, but what that told me was the admirals and generals might be expecting the Japs to try and retake the island. However, looking on the bright side, I thought back to several years before when I was a Boy Scout. Our motto was, 'Be Prepared.' Hopefully it was just a matter of preparing for the worst. Thinking about waves of Japanese soldiers coming at us with guns blazing was more than just somewhat worrisome. As a matter of fact, it was down right terrifying as we were only about five hundred strong.

Our tent was a sixteen-by-sixteen-foot pyramidal tent with a center pole, open sides, and a coral-sand floor. My tent mates were Bost, Meatnose Hillman, a gunner named Kurth, and a rifleman named Jolly. I was sure we would all be very happy there.

"Are we supposed to sleep in the sand?" Kurth asked.

"Hell no," answered Bost. "The supply tent is up and running. You can pick up a cot and a couple blankets. They got just about everything now, so whatever shit you lost getting ashore and during the battle can be replaced."

"I jettisoned everything getting ashore," Kurth said. "I replaced all the killing tools from the dead guys so I don't need any of that shit, but I damn sure could use some shaving gear and a tooth brush."

The CBs and Marines worked together around the clock moving supplies and equipment to several locations throughout the island. An area adjacent to the CB camp caught my attention because large amounts of supplies were being unloaded there. They seemed to be spending an inordinate amount of time building facilities to store and protect them. I decided I'd check it out more completely later.

Our main problem at that time was getting enough drinking water. We were being rationed two canteens per day, not even close to our needs. We were constantly on the lookout for ways to supplement our meager ration.

One night opportunity knocked. Hillman and I and four others were loading pallets of Coca-Cola onto a truck destined for the CB camp when the siren sounded, warning of an air attack. The working lights were doused and the CBs hauled ass to their assigned air-raid bunkers. We made a quick decision to hijack the Coke. The temptation was too great to pass up considering the short rations we were on. Hillman took the wheel and I jumped onto the running board to guide him through the dark night around bomb craters. We headed to the far side of the island as incoming bombs fell around us in sticks of seven or eight. After the first two hit it was possible to predict the line where the rest would fall. However, several planes were dropping bombs, making them impossible to track, but a load of Coke justified the risk. When we reached the end of the island we unloaded the cases of Coke in record time. Hillman drove the truck into the ocean and deep-sixed it over the edge of the coral reef, while the rest of us buried the loot in the coral sand. The all-clear sounded and we made our way back to our assigned duty post. No one was the wiser. Our project was successfully completed, and all evidence was out of sight.

With warm Coke in endless supply, the war took on a new, more pleasant light. Even filling sandbags in the hot sun became more tolerable. However, care needed to be taken in consuming the Coke, and the empties needed to be well hidden away from our camp. The CBs were damn pissed off about their loss and were offering substantial rewards for information leading to the recovery of their Coke. There was also mention of a lost truck.

In all fairness to the CBs, I must say they were a good bunch of guys. They were older men skilled in construction, as well as operating heavy equipment. They had a well-earned reputation for accomplishing impossible projects in unbelievably short periods of time. However, better provisions for their personal needs and comfort were envied and resented by the other units on the island but most particularly by the jarheads. I suppose what it came down to was the fact that their skills were so desperately needed they were elevated to an elite status. It became obvious to me that the Marines were expendable by reason of the way we were used at the landing where wave after wave of us were sent into an overwhelming barrage of firepower. We could be and were replaced as fast as our ranks were reduced.

After a few days of dieting on Coke and K-rations, most of the guys became afflicted with a severe case of gastro-intestinal troubles, commonly referred to as the GIs and the Coke was beginning to taste like medicine. Our ration of drinking water wasn't enough to last all day and our ill-gotten Coke filled that gap. However, we had a dilemma. We'd suffer from dehydration if we stopped drinking the Coke, or diarrhea if we kept guzzling. We kept guzzling, using our water mostly as a mouthwash to remove the taste of the Coke.

The Japs bequeathed to us a seagoing latrine. It was a rickety scaffold about thirty feet out over the ocean during low tide. At high tide it was about eight feet from the shoreline. The platform was approximately sixteen inches wide and twenty feet long, with a four-by-four-inch plank, elevated about fourteen inches above the platform to sit on. There were no guardrails or backrests. Access to the platform was gained by way of a walkway, which consisted of a series of unstable, warped two-by-twelve-inch planks.

While at Samoa we learned some Polynesian words, which we adapted to our inherited latrine. Fallei is Polynesian for house or hut, kai is excrement or dung. Kai-nippers were small crap-eating fish, and their name was a combination of Polynesian and Marine. Using a seagoing kai-fallei demanded balance, know-how, and urgency. The law of gravity and balance dictates that extending the posterior beyond the four-by-four plank would cause the body to be over-balanced to the rear, resulting in a fall backward into the sea. To counterbalance that dynamic, the sitter needed to lean forward as far as possible. In order for one person to get past another it was necessary for the sitter to assume an upright position, allowing the passer to squeeze by. Sitting upright, however, put the sitter in danger of falling backward. Guarding against that required advance planning. Therefore, prior to venturing out, the sitter needed to equip himself with a short rope with a large hook on the end. By looping the hook around the front edge of the platform, he was able to stabilize himself while sitting upright by holding onto the other end of the rope, allowing the passer-by to get by. Then both of them could relax, lean forward and watch the kai-nippers scramble after pre-processed K-rations.

Our platoon leader, Lieutenant Bakken, was told by Captain Hinshaw, the new company commander, that some of the men in his platoon were suspected of involvement in the big Coke heist. Duty required that he blow the whistle on them, but if he did he'd be reprimanded for lax discipline by allowing the theft to take place, and possibly lose his command. He didn't want to take that gamble, particularly after the men offered to share the swag with him. It wasn't long before he also was suffering the same fate as the others and was soon walking (or running, depending the degree of urgency) the plank with the best of us.

A disabled Jap tank lay half submerged about ten yards from the kai-fellei. Two or three dead Japs in the tank had been ripening for almost three weeks. One day the overpowering smell wafted in the general direction of the kai-fallei. The lieutenant decided it was time to eliminate that problem. He gave Private Katchouski a requisition for five gallons of diesel fuel and ordered him to dump it into the tank and torch if off as soon as possible. Two hours later, Katchouski had the tank fully engulfed when Lieutenant Bakken had to make another dash for the kai-fallei.

The lieutenant and some of the troops were settled down holding their ropes, alternating their interest between the kai-nippers and the burning tank. Black smoke and flames belched out of the open hatch, generating enough heat to make those perched on the kai-fallei uncomfortable enough to vacate their perch. As they were scrambling to get clear, a violent explosion shook the tank, followed in quick succession by several more. Then an ear-piercing blast from a shell in the breech of the .75 millimeter cannon on the tank blew away a section of the walkway, creating mass confusion. Those who hadn't fallen off the plank instinctively did what they were trained to do. They 'hit the deck'. In this case, however, there was no deck to hit so they all ended up floundering in the drink. The kai-nippers must have thought they had hit the jackpot as they swarmed in on the granddad of all meals. After a lot of thrashing around, the guys were able to convince the nippers, that wasn't the case, and they all made it to shore.

On the beach, panic created by the explosions and battle nerves of the troops had set in big time. They were convinced the Japs were coming back to retake the island.

"At ease, men!" Lieutenant Bakken screamed. "This is not a counter attack. The ammo in the tank blew up. That's all."

"Bullshit sir," shouted Private First Class Hendricks. "That was naval gunfire. The Japs are coming back."

It took a lot of convincing, but Bakken finally got them calmed down.

"I've had enough of that goddamn kai-fallei. We're going to build a real 'head' on the beach," Lieutenant Bakken declared.

"Can't do it, sir," Hendricks said. "We've tried to dig a crapper several times but the coral keeps sliding back in the hole. The sides won't hold up."

"Men, one of the things I learned in college was that for every problem there's a solution. If that's the only thing holding up constructing a real head, we need to come up with a solution."

"You're right, lieutenant," Adkins said. "I like the way you think, and I respect what you learned in college, so what kinda' solution you think we should come up with?"

"Use the boards from the kai-fallei to keep the coral from caving in," Bakken said.

"How we gonna to do all that without tools and nails?" Louzinski asked.

"I'll give you signed requisitions for whatever is required to complete this job. We need to get moving on this, men. As you can see, what's left of the kai-fallei can only accommodate one sitter and he'll have to swim both ways."

Two days later the major work was finished. We had dug a trench seven feet deep, ten feet long, and two feet wide, using the boards from the kai-fallei to keep the sides from caving in. We still needed to build a five-hole cover to prevent falling in backwards. Another problem we could do nothing about was that at high tide the trench took in four feet of water.

Unbeknownst to us at the time, we were being investigated by our company commander, Captain Hinshaw. Somehow, rumors persisted that members of our platoon were the culprits responsible for the theft of the CB's Coke. He must've had spies watching our movements because he was aware of a hole being dug, and assumed it was to bury the stolen Coke. That mistaken assumption would cost him dearly.

The all-out effort to install the big guns and radar was the number-one priority for us. We also stood security watches every night, and spent seemingly endless hours filling sandbags. Marine jargon for filling sandbags was 'strumming the banjo,' because our trenching tool, if one used a modicum of imagination, resembled a banjo.

Jap air raids were an ongoing event saturating the island with five-hundred-pound bombs, taking a toll on our ranks. Burying the dead became an everyday chore we needed to fit into our schedule. After we installed our big guns the raids became less frequent, but before we had a chance to become complacent we were blessed with a new method of killing and mayhem.

One night the moon came up like a beautiful big pumpkin illuminating the battle-scarred landscape. Ragged palm trees, upended trucks, blown-up tanks, and destroyed aircraft at weird angles merged to produce eerie silhouettes. Looking out to sea, a golden moonbeam produced a silken path that led directly to shore. Possibly the bombers would use it to guide them in. On a night such as that we could usually expect a delivery.

Sure enough, shortly after midnight while manning the long-range radar I saw several blips on the screen. I blew the siren, signaling to all on the island that the first wave of bombers were on their way. That was my first stint on the radar screen, since Reznik and I had conned our way out of scout/sniper and into the radar division while battle training at Samoa. Searchlights pierced the sky, looking for and locking onto the tiny reflective spots several thousand feet above. The big anti-aircraft guns opened up and flashes appeared near the planes. A few seconds later the muffled pop-pop-pop of the exploding anti-aircraft shells reached the ground. We expected the usual earth-shaking explosions of five-hundred-pound bombs, but instead the sky lit up in a blinding flash. A huge umbrella of white-hot particles slowly descended on the island. Phosphorus bombs! We had been told this could happen, but still it came as a shock. We knew if any phosphorus landed on us it would burn into our skin until the flesh sealed off the oxygen supply. Only a few of the dugouts or bunkers were covered. For the others there was no protection. The search for a piece of tin or anything to protect against the deadly phosphorus became a life-saving effort for those in the open.

The worst was yet to come as the next wave of bombers dropped 'daisy cutters.' A long plunger detonated the bomb a few feet above the ground, creating a flat trajectory, which cut the men down after being driven from their foxholes by the phosphorus.

There was a mad rush to reach the protection of the harbor. A few already burning with phosphorus were screaming for a corpsman. However, there was nothing a corpsman could do as the phosphorus had to be dug out under water at a later more convenient time.

Those who reached the harbor before the daisy cutters detonated and who hadn't been hit by phosphorus weren't affected, but those unable to reach the water were cut down and killed or wounded.

When it was over I sounded the all-clear and the wounded were carried to the field hospital, writhing and screaming in agony as the chemicals burned into their flesh. It was a ghastly sight. Several died that night, too badly burned to be saved. Many died in their foxholes, or trying to run from the horror raining down on them. They were left where they lay until morning, to be dealt with by Graves Registration.

It was my good fortune to have been inside the protection of the radar trailer during that raid.

While the phosphorus bombing raid was going on another incident was taking place. Captain Hinshaw was in the area of the new kai-fallei looking for evidence of the stolen Coke. He was looking for the hole he was certain the Coke was being buried in. He did indeed find the hole in the excitement of the phosphorus bombing. While looking up he stepped back and stumbled into the recently dug outhouse. There he was, splashing about in four feet of water and a considerable amount of enlisted men's crap. How humiliating for him.

After the raid, Privates Swartz and Riley walked over to the facility with every intention of answering a call to nature. As they prepared to sit down they heard a shout from below "Get me out of here!" The voice startled Swartz, and in his haste he slipped and fell in, joining Captain Hinshaw.

"Who's there?" Riley asked.

"Never mind who. Just get me the hell out of here,"

"Me too," Swartz said.

"If I'm going to help you out, I need to know who I'm helping. How do I know you're not a Jap spy."

"I'm Captain Hinshaw. Now get me out of here."

"Sir, what are you doing in our crapper?"

"I fell in, dammit."

Riley innocently said, "Sir, the crapper wasn't finished. If you wanted to use it, you should have waited till it was finished."

"I wasn't going to use it." Hinshaw snapped back. "Now get me out of here."

"Me too," Swartz pleaded.

"Sir," Riley answered with a hint of indignation, "we didn't build this crapper for the officers to use as a foxhole."

"Damnit, I wasn't going to use it as a foxhole, I fell in accidentally. Now find a rope and get me out of here. That's an order."

"Don't know where I might find a rope at this time of night. Maybe Lieutenant Bakken will have some ideas about what to do."

"No, don't do that. The officers don't have to know about this. Just get some of the troops and please hurry back."

Riley figured he had pushed it far enough. He rounded up a couple of the guys and rescued the captain, as well as Private Swartz.

CHAPTER 5

GARRISON DUTY

Part 2

There was no fresh water on the island, but the CBs had an evaporation machine which removed the salt, converting it to water suitable for showering. Fresh-water showers were out of the question for us as we had no such machine, and I was never sure if our officers or any other units on the island had them. In hindsight, my best guess, based on the other inequities, was that they did. We were issued saltwater soap and directed to the harbor. Saltwater bathing was a frustrating experience as I had learned on our journey from the States to Samoa as well as from Samoa to Tarawa. It's impossible to work up a lather and it leaves your skin dry and itching as opposed to that great feeling you get from a regular shower or from a bath. The best I can say about saltwater bathing is that it's only slightly better than nothing. The alternative was not bathing, which wasn't an acceptable option, considering the extreme heat and our less than pristine living conditions.

Someone once said, 'Necessity is the mother of invention.' Through our resourcefulness we managed to accumulate rainwater from the door flaps and the sagging top of our tent, which we funneled into a fifty-gallon gasoline drum. It was contaminated with oil from the tent and gasoline from the drum, but we could use it to wash our clothes and our hands. It was definitely a step in the right direction.

That effort went to hell the first week. There seemed always to be some self-centered son-of-a-bitch bent on screwing things up for everyone. Joe Almiedo was one such person. Kurth was the major mover in the fresh-water recovery program, so he was particularly upset when Almiedo decided to take a bath in the drum of semi-fresh rainwater. Kurth connected with a roundhouse right to the mouth, knocking Joe and the drum to the ground, where Kurth proceeded to roll him in the muddied coral sand until he was unrecognizable.

A week prior, Dirty Red McKrekin was treated in a like manner. He smelled like rotted guts because he refused to wash his filthy body. The guys in his tent gave him a brush scrub, which removed much of the crud as well as a good amount of his hide. His tent mates told him if he didn't take a trip to the harbor every day with a bar of saltwater soap and wash his disgusting body they'd kill him. They meant it, and he knew it.

Later, the water problem was resolved when a water trailer was brought in and centrally located to serve the occupants of four tents. This was definitely a good-news thing because now we'd have plenty of drinking water and could leave the unused Coke buried. Best of all, we could take a douche in fresh water. A douche in Marine jargon is a bath in a helmet full of water. Compared to saltwater bathing it's like going to heaven without dying. I never thought I'd ever be grateful for the opportunity to take a bath in a helmet.

During another air raid a five-hundred-pound bomb landed uncomfortably close to the foxhole I was in. The force of the explosion sent parts of a sandbag in my direction, driving one of the corners into my mouth with such force I couldn't remove it. I was in complete panic. I had sand in my eyes, my mouth and down my throat, causing me to strangle. I could barely breathe through my nose as it also had sand in it. I desperately fought the urge to vomit, knowing instinctively that it would cause more problems, because it would have no place to go. I needed help and in full panic leaped from my hole and headed in what I thought was the direction of sickbay.

Bost jumped out after me, yelling, "Get down, Olson. What the fuck are you trying to do, get yourself killed?"

The bombs were still falling, which is what he was yelling about, but that wasn't my immediate concern. I was gagging and retching and couldn't breathe or open my eyes and I was trying not to vomit. I couldn't tell him what was wrong, but when he saw my dilemma he grabbed my arm and directed me to sickbay.

Fortunately for me the corpsman immediately sized up the urgency of my problem and skillfully pried the obstacle loose and removed it from my mouth. He pushed a bucket of water my way, and I spent the next several minutes puking and hacking and blowing sand out of my mouth and nose. He led me to a table where he had placed a pan of water and I was able to flush the sand out of my eyes. My teeth were knocked loose and my mouth was bleeding. (All these years later those same teeth are still loose.) Otherwise I was OK, but many times since have relived that experience in dreams, jumping out of bed in claustrophobic panic, gasping for air.

CHAPTER 6

GARRISON DUTY

Part 3

The CBs had been erecting living quarters, galleys, mess halls, and showers for the Marine Corps Officers, the Air Corps pilots and personnel, as well as for themselves. The tents they were putting up had a wood frame with a peaked roof and a wood deck with screened sides. We assumed they would start building similar structures for us when they finished the others so we could move out of our miserable tents. We also figured they'd build a galley for us so we could start eating real food. We hoped we'd start receiving beer rations. None of those things happened. Our only luxury was the water trailer. I suppose we should have been grateful for that but we weren't; not while the others on the island were enjoying the amenities we were deprived of. This had become a matter of deep concern and resentment, and the source of serious discussion. Bost and some of the other sergeants got together and submitted a grievance to First Sergeant Mueller, who said he'd pass our grievance on to the platoon leaders.

"Well, OK." said Kurth. "So when we gonna start getting beer and decent chow?"

"The first sergeant said he'd pass the word onto the platoon leaders." Bost answered. "That's all I know; we'll just have to wait and see what happens."

"Incidentally, Olson," Bost continued, "your buddy Reznik is off the hospital ship. I met him when I was in the First Sergeant's office, and I made arrangements to have him move in here with us."

"No kidding, Bost, that's great news. I'm glad to hear that. When is he going to show up?" Not waiting for an answer, I said, "Maybe I'll just go on down and help him with his gear. You know I saw him when he was heading for the hospital ship. He was all bloody and bandaged up and he looked like shit. I figured they'd send him home—he looked that bad."

After he got squared away we spent some time exchanging war stories. There was no doubt he'd had it worse than I had. I know I was lucky to get tagged by Major Schmidt to protect his command post, not that it was a stroll in the park, but it damn sure was better than what Reznik and those others did.

"You guys ready for this?" Reznik asked as he broke out a tin of sick bay alky. "I requisitioned this when nobody was looking."

Kurth said. "You better believe we're ready for that, and I got just the right stuff to cut it with."

Kurth reached into his sea bag and came up with a large can of grapefruit juice, referred to as battery acid, the perfect mix for one-hundred-fifty-proof alcohol.

"I requisitioned this a couple weeks ago, just in case."

"Just in case of what?" Reznik asked.

"Just in case opportunity knocked and I, or someone else, was able to acquire some torpedo juice or a tin of alky. It seems you're that someone else."

"Break it out, Dude, and we'll get drunk," Reznik said.

"Reznik, I see you got a pretty bad limp," I said. "What happened, did you get shot or stop some shrapnel, or what?"

"Glad you asked, Olson. I been wanting to tell you about that. What happened was, we was advancing on one of them cement bunkers that had two thirty-calibers that was keeping us pinned down. Me and Tex was about ready to slip up from their side, and drop a grenade in the slits where the guns were. We were in the protection of a disabled tank and ready to make our move and guess what? We both got shot from behind, both of us in the leg, and both of us at the same time. We went down right away and turned to see where the shots came from so we could return the favor but there was nobody there. We knew the Jap that shot us was right behind us because we heard the shots and they was close."

"Don't tell me." Bost said, "It was a trap-door foxhole, I'll bet."

"You're right, Bost. That's what it was, and the funny thing was we knew damn well it was right there, but we couldn't see no sign of it."

"So what did you do?" I asked.

"We didn't do nothin cause we couldn't see it, but a guy with us saw the whole thing because he was behind it. He slipped up and opened the hatch and dropped a grenade in and hauled ass. We flattened out so we wouldn't catch any shrapnel and that was the end of that- just one more dead Jap."

"How did the guy that dropped the grenade know how to open the hatch?" I asked.

"There you go again Olson, getting all technical. How the hell would I know how he knew how to open the fucking hatch? He just knew. Maybe there was a sign on it that said 'open here'."

"Anyway, Olson, I got a question for you," Reznik said. "How did you get off the Higgins Boat alive at the fucked-up landing when all the guys were getting killed?"

"Good question. I jumped off the side of the ramp and ended up in a bomb crater and fucking near drowned. But what happened to you?"

"I jumped off the side of the ramp, too, but I didn't see you and I didn't fall into a bomb crater."

"That's because you probably went off the left side. I went off on the right side. Anyway, I'm glad you made it."

"Bost, what do you hear from the first sergeant?" Jolly asked. "I saw you talking to him this morning. When we gonna get a galley and some decent chow and a beer ration and that other stuff?"

Kurth said, "yeah, I thought you and Bernham and some of the other sergeants was gonna get something going for us. What's the deal, when will we get beer?"

"First Sergeant Mueller said we'd get a galley as soon as the CBs could work it in. He thought they'd get to it in a couple days," Bost said.

"How about beer? When we gonna get beer?" Kurth asked again.

"I don't know, Kurth. It don't sound too good about the other shit. He said he'd talk to them again. I know he wasn't telling me everything," Bost answered.

"What's that supposed to mean?" Hillman asked. "Are we gonna get beer or not? And what do you mean he wasn't telling you everything?"

"Bost, I think you need to tell us all you know," I said. "What's going on?"

"I don't know any more than you. I told you everything he said. It's what he didn't say that bothers me."

"What didn't he say?" I asked.

"Mueller was evasive and he wouldn't look at me. I think they turned him down and he just didn't want to say that. I don't think we're gonna get anything from them. Maybe a galley and better chow— that's it."

No one said anything for a moment. That was a shocking revelation, and it was going to take a while for it to soak in. The power and control they had over us scared the crap right out of me. To think that something as simple as a bottle of beer, which meant so much to us, could be withheld at their whim was hard to accept, particularly when we figured all the others on the island were getting beer.

Reznik spoke up. "This is bullshit. We put our lives on the line, and the few of us lucky enough to live through all that shooting deserve to be treated better than this. I wouldn't say a goddamn word if everyone here was in the same boat, but that's not the way it is. Everybody on this fucking rock is getting beer except us."

"What's driving me nuts is, why? Riley said. "Why are we being treated this way? What did we do that we weren't supposed to do or what were we supposed to do that we didn't do that would cause them to fuck us over like this?"

"None of those things, Riley," Bost said. "We didn't do nothn' we weren't supposed to and we damned sure did everything we were asked to do. We killed Japs and we fought our asses off.

I heard two thousand Marines got killed, and more than that got wounded. Our chances were no better or no worse than them guys. It was just shit-house luck that we lived and they didn't."

"So how come these fuck-heads are treating us like we're a piece of shit?" Hillman asked.

"I'm pretty sure I know the answer," Bost said.

"Bost, if you got answers we sure as hell want to hear them, Reznik said.

"When they sent the battalion to New Zealand, almost all the officers went, too. The replacement officers came directly from the States or from units that hadn't been in combat yet, except Lieutenant Smith and a couple other junior officers."

"That's it," I said. "Why didn't I think of that? You hit it right on the nose, Bost. That's probably what it's all about."

"I don't know that I agree with you guys or not about why we're getting screwed over, and I don't think I care. I just want to be treated equal to the CB grunts and the Air Corps guys, and all the others," Reznik said.

"What difference does it make if they're non-combatants or not? We're all Marines ain't we?" Kurth added.

Jolly said, "Kurth you're right. We're all Marines, and it shouldn't make any difference if they've seen combat yet or not. That's what's making our situation so damn difficult. We've lived up to the code all the way, and they're letting us down."

"Bost gave us something to think about, as far as I'm concerned," I said. "I agree with his idea about the new officers, and I also agree with Reznik's thinking that it doesn't make any difference what the reasons are. What's important is we're getting fucked-over big time, and we need to try to do something about it. I don't think there's anything in the code that says I should lie on my back like a dog and say, 'beat me.' I hope Bost is wrong and they'll re-think they're position and everything will work out. That's what I hope. What I think is, I think we're screwed."

CHAPTER 7

GARRISON DUTY

Part 4

Jolly said, "Well, I don't know about you guys, but I'm ready to go over and steal their beer."

"Go over where and steal whose beer?" Reznik asked.

"Go over to the CB supply yard and take their goddamn beer."

"That's a hell of an idea, Jolly," I said.

"Do you know where the beer is?" Bost asked.

"Hell yes," Jolly answered. "It was in a warehouse without sides, and if it's still there we can walk away with as much of it as we want if there isn't an armed guard, if that's what you're getting at."

"Yeah that's what I'm getting at," Bost said.

Reznik jumped up and said, "Shit, guys, that's it. We'll steal their fucking beer."

Kurth was all over that idea. "Let's all go over right now and each of us carry back a case. What are we waiting for?"

"Kurth, we can't do that. We gotta figure this thing out," Reznik said. "Now I got an idea. Tell me what you think of this: there's two of us right here who do security watch in the radar shack. We sound the alarm and the CBs haul ass for their air raid bunker. That's when we make our move. We go over there and walk off with their beer. What do you think about that idea?"

"That's a real bright idea," Jolly said. "We just walk over there and carry their beer away while bombs are dropping all around us."

"No, no, Jolly, you don't get the picture; we sound the alarm when the Japs *aren't* coming, but we're the only ones that know that," Reznik said.

"Oh, OK, I get it," Jolly said. "Then when our beer requisition party is over, whoever is on the radar sounds the all clear, and the CBs and everyone crawl out of their air raid hole and we drink beer all night. Is that what you're trying to say?"

"Yeah, you got it, Jolly. That's what I'm trying to say."

Bost, turning toward me, asked, "How many false alarms can we get away with before they get wise, Olson?"

"I don't think that'll be a problem," I answered. "With all the air activity around here, we get false readings all the time, so if we space ours out we should be OK."

"Anyone got an idea how we should start?" Kurth asked.

Jolly spoke up. "I think we should do a dry run and work out the details."

"Good idea," I said. "We probably should work out a circuitous route between where the beer is and our camp."

"That's a hell of an idea, Olson," Reznik said. "I definitely think we should do that. Olson what does circuit us route mean, or whatever it was you just said?"

"Circuitous. I said circuitous. It means a round-about route from the beer to our tent instead of a straight line."

"Well, OK, I agree. I think that's the route we oughta take. What do you guys think?" Reznik asked.

Jolly jumped in with his say. "We don't want to get too circuitous here because, as you all know, Marines are on security watch all over the place when an alarm is sounded. We're liable to circuitous ourselves right into some Marine's foxhole and get our asses shot off."

"Yeah, your right," Bost said. "So we need to rethink the circuitous thing and plan our route around the gun emplacements and foxholes."

We decided to stash the loot in a blown-up Jap tank near our tent, because we didn't think it would be a good idea to have it in our quarters in case there was an inspection. A problem we couldn't get around was, not knowing when the Japs would pay a visit. They didn't come every night and sometimes they came more than once a night. We didn't want to be out in the open stealing beer when bombs were falling, particularly those goddamn phosphorus bombs. We didn't know when the bombs would fall and it was pretty hard to make plans when we didn't have all the facts. Jolly suggested we call over and try to get their bombing schedule, and that was a good idea except for one thing. We didn't have their number. It was decided we should wait until a night when I was on the radar and the Japs hadn't shown up. That's as close to a plan as we could come up with.

At 0230 on a moonlit night I passed the word that I was going to blow the siren in five minutes. This was to be a dry run. I sounded the alarm and as expected everyone on the island hauled ass to their assigned shelter, and the midnight requisition squad headed toward the CB warehouse. I had no sooner sounded the alarm when three blips appeared on the screen moving in our direction. I had no way of getting word to Reznik and the others to abort the operation.

When they got to the CB warehouse, I learned later, they changed their plans from a dry run to, in Rezniks' words, a wet run. They each grabbed a case and headed for the Jap tank. Just then the bombs started falling and the big guns came to life, and as Jolly described it later, they were up shit creek without a paddle not knowing what to do. Actually, they were already committed and had no choice but to follow through. They wended a new circuitous route to the Jap tank, deposited their loot and hung there until I sounded the all clear.

At 0600 when my watch ended, I headed for 'home,' anxious to see the guys and find out how our dry run had turned out. It was better than a dry run and it was obviously a success, but no one was talking. Everyone except Bill Gripp was passed out, and Pabst Blue Ribbon beer bottles were strewn about the tent.

"How did everything go last night?" I asked.

"Beats me," Gripp said. "I just got off the mid-to-six watch same as you. I was on the .50 caliber. That was a pretty good fireworks show. We shot one of them down. By the way, Olson, I thought we were gonna raid the CB beer when the Japs weren't flying."

"I didn't know they were coming until after I had sounded our false alarm, which turned out to be a real-thing alarm."

"Help me wake up these ass-holes, Gripp; we're gonna be in a load of trouble if someone walks in and sees these beer bottles and these jarheads passed out like this. They might be smart enough to put two and two together and come up with four."

"We better hurry because you and me gotta work together filling bags. Sergeant Bernham told me to grab you when you came off watch."

We shook the drunks awake and told them they needed to hide the bottles, then headed out to fill sandbags.

Because Tarawa's a mere four degrees off the equator the temperature often reaches one hundred thirty degrees during the day. Filling sandbags is a miserable job because there's no shade, so we arranged to do that job early in the morning to beat the heat. We went to where we were to work but nature called and I told Bill Gripp I'd be back in a minute. I was about fifty feet away when I heard a loud explosion and felt the pressure of a blast, as particles of dead coral hit my back. I turned to see Bill Gripp standing but slowly caving in toward the ground. His head had been sliced in half by the edge of his trenching tool, which had hit and detonated a Jap land mine.

He was next to me one minute alive and the next minute he was dead, his head split in two. I was never going to get used to that shit, I remember thinking. He was an older guy, probably about twenty-six, possibly married, maybe had kids.

"Life goes on," said Reznik later that night in our tent. "He ain't the first jarhead to get blowed up, and he damned sure ain't gonna be the last."

Life had improved for us as the promised mess hall was completed and we were getting better chow, not great, but better. We were able to make one more trip to the CB beer hoard before they got wise and started posting guards. That put us out of business, at least for awhile, and forced us to moderate our drinking by setting up a rationing system. We limited ourselves to two beers each per day, which was almost the right amount to take the edge off of the deplorable life we were living.

Our raids on the CB beer supply paled in terms of ingenious illegalities when compared to Private Glutz and his shenanigans.

CHAPTER 8
GARRISON DUTY

Part 5

Private Joe Glutz was the battalion screw-up. He was the only guy who didn't talk about women and booze. As a matter of fact he was too dumb to carry on a conversation of any kind. The guys wouldn't let him play poker because they had to explain the rules every hand. No one could figure out how he had survived the assault on the island, though there were a number of theories. The one that made the most sense to me had him hiding out in one of our destroyed tanks for three days, showing up when the shooting stopped.

In any event he seemed incapable of performing the simplest of tasks, and Captain Hinshaw was at a loss as to what to do with him. Somehow he managed to screw up every task assigned him. He said he could drive a truck but wrecked it in half an hour. As a mess cook he put soap powder in a kettle of C rations. He was assigned the job of cleaning the officers' tents but fell asleep while smoking and burned down the adjutant's tent and all its contents.

One day, First Sergeant Mueller had a brilliant idea. He suggested they assign Glutz to the garbage dump, give him a pad of paper and instruct him to give one slip to the truck drivers each time they dumped a load. Unbeknownst to him this served no purpose but provided him with a job he thought to be meaningful. The captain was delighted with the idea and they put it into effect immediately.

The war had moved farther north, and the Japs quit bombing the island. Life settled down to the dull routine of garrison duty, and the troops continued playing poker and talking about women but not about booze. At times they were seen walking around with a smug smile on their face; some staggered a bit. At night there was singing in some tents.

Captain Hinshaw and the other officers knew the enlisted ranks were getting liquor but had no idea how that was happening. They were probably more disturbed because they weren't getting any themselves. This reverse discrimination was unheard of in the corps, and it had to be stopped. Hinshaw assigned two non-coms to find out how the men were getting liquor, but the investigation came to naught since those assigned to investigate were among the consumers. They had no intention of killing this goose. They were ingenious in keeping the investigation alive by creating non-existent but believable scenarios, satisfying the captain that progress was being made and that answers would be forthcoming.

A week or so later, when Captain Hinshaw was in the Post Office tent he observed the winning poker players buying hundred dollar money orders. In the line was Private Glutz with a fistful of money. The captain thought it strange that Glutz would have a large sum of money since he was too stupid to play poker let alone be a big winner at the game. The only other activity that could produce large profits was selling Jap souvenirs to soldiers and sailors, but Glutz wasn't in a location where he could do that. Puzzled by this unexplainable event the captain asked the mail clerk if Private Glutz had sent much money home and was told Glutz came in once a week to purchase money orders and had sent home five hundred dollars that day.

That was a mystery he intended to solve and very astutely concluded that the two, non-com's he had assigned to investigate this mystery were probably never going to do so. They might even be involved, he figured. He summarily dismissed them from their special duty assignment and decided to put his two best platoon leaders on the case. He instructed Lieutenants Kawalski and Johnson to spy on Glutz, thinking there might be a connection between his, as yet unexplained wealth and the source of the liquor. A week later they reported that they had observed the trucks dumping their loads of trash. On close inspection they noticed yeast and large amounts of sugar as well as prunes being set aside. Cleverly hidden within the piles of refuse they found several items that supported Captain Hinshaws suspicions.

Even though there was an acute water shortage, Glutz had a water trailer at his disposal and a fuel-oil-fired galley stove hooked up to homemade distillery equipment, and two. twenty-gallon lister bags full of fermenting prunes. Lister bags are rubberized canvas water bags, used by the CBs on construction sites. Glutz had a first-class moonshine operation producing large amounts of very powerful white lightning from fermented prunes. Captain Hinshaw was in a quandary about what to do. He was reluctant to shut him down because this could be a source of liquor for the officers since they weren't getting any from the States. However, being a career officer, he lived by the book and knew he had to put Glutz out of business. He figured out a way to satisfy both objectives. He ordered First Sergeant Mueller to have the distillery dismantled, confiscate all the finished product, and deliver it to the officers mess, a small amount to be used as evidence in his case. He then instructed him to draw up papers for a summary court martial naming Private Joseph Glutz defendant.

A thorough investigation needed to be conducted to support his case. He assigned Lieutenant Kawalski to investigate the means of production, which included the source of the sugar and yeast as well as the equipment used to distill the liquor. He was to submit a brief summary on the different steps taken. Lieutenant Johnson was to investigate the distribution and sale of the liquor. Captain Hinshaw would investigate the Post Office records.

A week later Kawalski reported that the main ingredient was cooked prunes, and any uneaten fermentable food, and large amounts of sugar and yeast. The necessary equipment was a cook stove, metal containers, copper tubing, and lister bags. The prunes and other food went through a fermenting process in the lister bags and was then cooked and processed into the finished product.

The difficult part of his investigation was learning how Glutz was able to secure everything needed. He concluded that the truck drivers were the key. They were the ones who made the deals to secure the material and equipment. Kawalski learned that they made deals with the Army Air Corps enlisted personnel and the Navy aircraft repair guys, and of course some of the Marine platoons. The motivation was the promise of liquor, and profit from the sale of the product.

Lieutenant Johnson had run into a complex network of distribution and sale, which started with the truck drivers. Glutz produced the liquor and the drivers sold it, turning over half of what they collected to Glutz. They were all independent businessmen selling the product not only for cash but trading it to other Marines for Jap souvenirs, which they sold to newly arrived soldiers and sailors passing through.

Captain Hinshaw's investigation of postal records indicated Glutz had sent home over twenty thousand dollars since he and the First Sergeant had so brilliantly solved the Private Glutz problem by sending him to the garbage dump to hand out meaningless slips of paper to the truck drivers.

He correctly concluded that if he was to go forward with a trial he would have to file charges against not only Glutz but all the miscreants involved. That was not a course he intended to take because to do so would expose the fact that he had been negligent in allowing this outrageous behavior to take place behind his back. It very well could be the end of his career. He wasted no time canceling the court martial procedure and ordering the First Sergeant to dispose of all the equipment into the harbor, including all the liquor.

How could everyone have been so wrong about Private Glutz? Was he really as stupid as he seemed or did he brilliantly create that image?

CHAPTER 9

GARRISON DUTY

Part 6

A bone of contention was the tents we were living in. The Marines were the only ones not provided with peaked-roof, wood-frame tents with wood decks. Reznik broached that subject. He had the ability to rile the troops for or against anything, and his opening statement was so designed.

"I don't think I'm any better than any other ass-hole but I also figure there ain't no sonofabitch no better than me."

"What the hell got your bowels in an uproar?" I asked.

"Look at these goddamn tents we got, than look at the tents everyone else got. Don't you think I have a right to be pissed about that?"

"Hell yes you got a right to be pissed; but what's new? You got a right to be pissed about a lotta things, but so what? This is what you signed up for, so quit your goddamn bellyaching. Here, have a beer."

"I know what I signed up for," he said. "I signed up to fight this fucking war and kill Japs and whatever else I had to do, but I didn't sign up to be treated like I was a piece of shit. Thanks for the beer."

"Reznik, if you got an idea how we can get a better tent, you need to tell us about it or quit flapping your jaws," Bost said.

Jolly got up off his cot and staggered into the center pole holding our tent up, saying, "I got an idea how we can get a decent tent."

"If you're gonna talk, Jolly," Bost said, "maybe you better stay sitting before you knock down this poor excuse for a tent, which, bad as it is, is still better than nothing. But if you got an idea how we can get a better tent then let's hear about it, hoss."

"You guys have all seen the lumber stacked up in the CB supply area and, I heard some of it is already cut to the right size needed for the deluxe-model tent. What I think we ought to do is, I think we oughta just go over there and carry back the stuff we need to build our own tent."

Everyone agreed that was a good idea. In fact, we figured it was such a good idea we would have celebrated by having another beer bust that night except we didn't have any more beer. However, that didn't dampen our spirits about the new project under consideration. We decided to keep our plans simple because they generally went to shit anyway. We only needed a couple false-alarm air raids to get all the stuff to build our new tent. Jolly and Kurth agreed to reconnoiter the supply area during the day and pinpoint the required materials. One night when Reznik was on the radar screen we made our move. It worked out surprisingly well, and we were able to get everything in two raids.

Construction started immediately and took less than a week to complete. Our old sagging tent was taken down, and we enthusiastically moved in to our new quarters. We built a table for poker or letter writing, and extra shelves for personal stuff or a picture of our wife or girl friend, if we hadn't already been dumped. Over the entrance we attached a Jap skull to a pole, painted it red and placed it next to a sign with the name of our new home, "SACKRAT MANOR."

Reznik summed it all up when he said, "It don't get no better than this."

Life was better with our new tent. I wouldn't say enjoyable, it would take much more than a tent for that, but it was a great improvement. However, this utopia was soon to end. One day about ten days after the completion of our new quarters, the Sergeant of the

Guard unceremoniously burst into our new digs and shouted, "Ten-hut!" We all jumped up, bewildered by this uninvited intrusion, and stood stiffly at attention, staring to the front.

Captain Paige, the new company commander strode in, looked around, and after examining every detail of our quarters, said. "Fall in outside on the double."

We scrambled outside and formed a line. The Sergeant of the Guard marched us to an area where we joined a group of about ten other Marines standing at attention. I didn't figure out until later why they were there.

Captain Paige slapped his swagger stick across his thigh and said, "Men you did a fine job fixing up this tent. Of course you realize you're all subject to courts martial for stealing materials from the CBs. However, I've been told you're all combat Marines who fought gallantly here. I congratulate you for your courage and have decided to take that into consideration and not file procedures against you. However, I have no intention of allowing you to continue benefiting from your ill-gotten gains. You have exactly five minutes to remove your gear, form up around the tent, lift and move it to where you see that Air Corps officer standing. That's a direct order and I expect it to be dealt with as such. Carry on."

It became obvious why the other ten guys were there. They joined together with us and we carried our tent to the designated location as ordered. We positioned it with the opening facing the morning sun as directed and were summarily dismissed. The Air Corps officer was observed transferring a case of Old Crow from his jeep to Captain Paige's jeep.

We proceeded with the depressing task of erecting our old, sagging, patched-up tent, working in silence but not without strong feelings of hatred. Revenge was in order, and we intended to get some. Many ideas were put forth, most of which were eliminated as they included torture, murder, and the use of our Kabar knives for removal of certain body parts.

Reznik spoke up. "What I think we oughta do is, I think we oughta blackmail the sonofabitch."

"How do you plan on doing that?" Bost asked.

"Well, shit, Bost, I don't have a plan; I'm just the idea man. You guys figure out the details."

"What do you think, Olson?" Bost asked. "How does blackmail sound to you?"

"I like it, but I can't come up with a plan off the top of my head."

A couple days later it fell into place. The idea was to start a rumor that Captain Paige had ordered us to steal the building materials from the CBs and build the tent for the Air Corps officers. Part of our trumped-up story was that Captain Paige had been paid off with several cases of booze and we had received a case of Old Crow bourbon for our part in the escapade. It worked beautifully, thanks mostly to Sergeant Bost dropping a few innocent but telling remarks to the Duty Officer when he was assigned Sergeant of the Guard duties. It took just a few days for the scuttlebutt to reach Colonel Thompson, the battalion commander. Evidently he was able to verify enough facts to support the rumors. Captain Paige was immediately transferred to an advance combat unit in the Marshall Islands. Maybe he got a taste of combat. Maybe the sonofabitch got his ass shot off.

Was justice served? Yes, but only partially. There was still the matter of the Air Corps officers who had acquired Sackrat Manor by devious and unscrupulous, to say nothing of illegal means. We considered the tent to be ours, and had been stolen from us. We had every intention of stealing it back as soon as we could come up with a plan. To add insult to our loss, the Air Corps officers were using Sackrat Manor as an officers' club. They were hardcore drinkers who loved to party, and with their unlimited supply of stateside liquor did so nightly. They were loud and raucous, keeping us awake and depriving us of our rightful expectation of peace and quiet.

I had just gotten off a six-hour watch on the radar screen and was bone tired, needing serious sack time. The Air Corps guys were partying in their best form, louder than usual it seemed. I had been thinking about a way to get these bastards out of our lives, and decided tonight would be the perfect night to put my plan into action.

I woke Reznik and Hillman. "I've had enough of this crap. Here's the plan: Reznik, you get on one side of the tent, and, Hillman, you get on the other side. When you hear me shout 'banzai!' both of you squeeze off a clip into the air. I'll dump the powder out of a grenade and toss it in and holler 'banzai again. The plan worked perfectly. When the Air Corps guys heard the primer cap go off in the grenade they literally burst out of Sackrat Manor and took off running in all directions. Actually, the plan was much more successful than I had planned, which makes sense, since our plans seldom went according to plan. The island went on the alert, and the whole Marine battalion was kept up all night looking for the Jap soldiers who had attacked the Air Corps. It was rumored a detachment of Jap soldiers had parachuted in on a suicide mission to kill as many people as possible.

Scaring the Air Corps guys was a good thing because they never came near Sackrat Manor again.

Jolly said what we were all thinking; "Let's bring Sackrat Manor back home."

Nobody said anything for a minute, then Bost asked, "When you think we should do that, Jolly?"

"I hadn't thought about when, but since you asked, how about after evening chow?"

"I think after evening chow would be as good a time as any. How about the rest of you gyrenes? Are you ready to bring our home back home?"

Our remaining days on Tarawa were definitely more pleasurable, though in hind-sight, I'm fairly sure we didn't fool anyone. I believe they were fully aware of what we were capable of and decided, since our time there was nearly over anyway, not to push it.

CHAPTER 10

KAUAI

Our tour of duty at Tarawa ended. The U.S. Army took over as protectors of Betio, and as far as I was concerned they were welcome to it. We were loaded aboard a troop transport and taken to Hawaii. The destination was Kauai, but we docked at Pearl Harbor for a day. It felt good to be in a temperate climate; downright cold compared to Tarawa. Several ships of the destroyed American fleet still lay in their dismal glory, mired in the mud of the harbor. The salvageable battleships and other warships had been moved to the shipyard and made whole and were settling accounts in the many Naval battles in the Pacific.

I jumped ship and called my brother, Bob from a telephone on the dock. Bob was a corpsman attached to Naval Hospital #128 at Pearl Harbor. He managed a liberty pass, and we spent the afternoon together talking about home and swapping war stories. I told him about the lousy duty at Tarawa, and he got a kick out of the Joe Glutz story. I also told him about all the Jap souvenirs I had brought with me.

"What kind of stuff did you bring back, Denny?"

"Damnit, Bob, will you please not call me Denny? You know how I hate that name, and you damn sure haven't forgotten how many times I kicked your ass up there between your eyeballs for calling me that."

"Sorry, Bud, it's just that I always think of you as 'Denny'- just a habit I guess— and yeah, I do remember how many times you

59

kicked my ass, and my recollection is that it was once, not several times, as you seem to remember. Also, I don't think it would have happened that time if you hadn't blind-sided me."

"As usual, little brother, you're as full of shit as a Christmas turkey. I didn't blind-side you; I flat out kicked your ass."

"Yeah, you're right, you probably kicked my ass hundreds of times and I just don't remember. Anyway, what's the story on your souvenirs? What do you have?"

We went below and I dug out my prized collection. I had a couple Jap Mamba pistols, a Samurai sword, two .31 caliber rifles, and a lot of sen and yen notes, as well as other trade goods. Brother Bob was quite impressed.

"Why don't you let me take them with me? I'm a second-class petty officer, and sometimes I censor mail. I can package and mail them home for you."

That sounded like a hell of a deal. I was glad I didn't have to lug them around anymore and felt sure they would get home. We said goodbye and Bob left the ship loaded down with all my swag from Tarawa.

About six months later I got a letter from him telling me he had lost them all playing poker. I didn't know he played poker. Clearly he didn't play very well, as was evidenced by the loss of my very valuable souvenirs.

The following day the ship proceeded to the island of Kauai. We joined together with survivors of other Pacific campaigns and became the 2nd AAA Battalion of the 3rd Marine Division. We set up our camp on an old Hawaiian battleground. Skeletons of Hawaiian warriors were buried in shallow graves throughout the area, according to local history.

After setting up camp we were given liberty. It was rumored there was a slop-shoot in operation so we headed for the bus to Kapah. "What the hell's a sloop-shot?" Reznik asked.

"It's not 'sloop-shot,' Reznik. It's called a 'slop-shoot.'" Bost said.

"Whatever the hell you call it, what the fuck is it?"

"It's kinda like a beer bar. You'll see when we get there."

It turned out to be a thatch-covered structure set up with two-by-twelve-inch planks, eight feet long, sitting end to end on saw horses which served as the bar. The whole thing was about ten yards long. We arrived at 1140 hours and became part of a crowd of about two hundred thirsty Marines. It was a commercial enterprise run by natives. There were hundreds of cases of Royal Premium beer stacked up behind the 'bar,' and about thirty bar tenders ready for action. At 1155 hours an MP sergeant jumped up on a box and announced: "You men can have all the beer you can drink, one beer at a time. If me or one of my men catch anyone, and that means just one of you, with more than one beer in front of you, we'll shut er down. In any event, the bar closes at 1300 hours, so drink fast and don't forget the rules."

The object was to chug-a-lug a beer. As soon as a bartender saw a hand reach out he grabbed the empty and replaced it with a full bottle. There was no time to take a leak, smoke a cigarette, shoot the breeze, or do a damn thing except down as many beers as possible in the allotted time. It was actually pretty crappy beer. If it had been cold it probably would have been acceptable, but warm it tasted like ol' mule sweat. After half an hour of steady drinking one guy got a little too relaxed and forgot to hand the bartender his empty. One of the MPs spotted him with a beer in his hand and an empty on the bar in front of him.

"That's it! Shut er down!" he shouted.

In a typical Marine protest, the MPs were told to fuck off. The MPs did however have the authority to shut down the bar and the MP Sergeant had every intention of using that authority to its fullest. He and his loyal troops began pushing the drinkers out of the slop-shoot. Big mistake! The Marines, mild mannered as they were, did protest vigorously. They proceeded to pummel the kindly MPs to a pulp. As a parting gesture of good will, the MP Sergeant was hung by his wrists from a low cross arm on a telephone pole.

"I can't drink it now, but tomorrow it'll probably taste pretty good," Reznik said as we boarded the bus back to camp.

"What the hell are you talking about?" I asked.

"While you ass-holes were thrashing them MPs, I went behind the bar, me and a few others, and stuffed as many bottles as we could in our pockets. I got five or six."

The R&R was much needed and appreciated as we were able to catch up on our sleep and take non-stop hot showers as well as enjoying the great climate. I had given up any idea of prolonged duty there as it was made clear we could look forward to another combat mission when the destroyed equipment and the heavy loss of personnel killed and wounded had been replaced. That didn't stop me from daydreaming and I created several scenarios. One was that they would forget about us and we would spend the rest of the war there. Another was that they would send us to Samoa for more training. Then there was the one that sent Reznik and me stateside for advanced radar training. My favorite was that the Japanese surrendered after the trouncing they received at Tarawa and we all went home. Daydreaming was about as meaningful as shoveling smoke but the alternative was facing the reality of another combat mission such as Tarawa. I preferred daydreaming.

William 'Bill' Rubans, better known in the Corps as Bobwire Bill, had been recuperating in a Naval hospital at Pearl from wounds received in the Guadalcanal campaign. He was promoted to Master Gunnery Sergeant and sent to Kauai as Top Sergeant in the Second AAA Battalion to rebuild our unit and train replacements in preparation for the next battle.

Bill Rubans was preceded by his reputation, probably colored but supposedly based on fact. He was an interesting character who had been in the Marine Corps since 1917. He was fifteen when he enlisted, so the story goes, but lied about his age so he could fight in World War One. In France while charging German trenches he got hung up on barbed wire in no man's land and was unable to get loose. He hung there while machine gun and rifle fire, mortar projectiles and artillery whizzed by and exploded all around him. During the night he managed to untangle himself and return to his platoon in the trenches. Other then a few scratches from the barbs he was unhurt. That incident was the start of the legend that forever tagged him, 'Bobwire Bill'.

He performed many heroic acts and was decorated by the governments of France, England, Belgium, and the United States. At war's end he had a chest full of medals, including three Purple Hearts, but never received the Good Conduct Medal. When World War One, "The war to end all wars" was over, he shipped over, and was assigned guard duty in various diplomatic legations throughout the world. Prior to and during the attack on Pearl Harbor he was on embassy duty in Manila. When war was declared against Japan, Bill declared open season on the Japanese. He went over to their embassy and started a minor war, shooting six guards and receiving two slugs during the fracas. He was flown to the States to recuperate and received another Purple Heart.

He was a platoon sergeant in the Second Marine Division during the campaign at Guadalcanal, and in various battles demonstrated outstanding leadership and courage and was awarded more medals, including another Purple Heart.

All the Marines in the battalion held him in high esteem and were glad to train under, and learn from him. However, he wasn't accorded the same respect from the officers. His command presence made 2nd Lieutenants and even Captains cringe. His profanity could put drill instructors to shame, and he seemed to have the ability to curse between syllables.

He proceeded to whip the 2nd AAA into shape for an inspection by a two star general scheduled for Wednesday. On Tuesday the battalion formed up for rehearsal. I was in charge of the brig at that time so was excused from the formation. My duty was to oversee the prisoners in policing up the area, which needed to be shipshape for the occasion the following day.

Tuesday, nine hundred officers and men as well as the band, all in starched khaki, stood at attention in formation waiting for the rehearsal to begin. The band had just completed the playing of "Stars and Stripes Forever." All eyes shifted across the parade ground to where old Bobwire had wandered leading Yardbird, his English Bulldog. He staggered up to the flagpole and Yardbird lifted his leg and gave the pole a quick squirt. Bobwire looked at the little dog for a moment, than zipped down his fly and proceeded to water the pole. He must have been drinking a lot of beer as it took a long time for him to finish. He zipped up and staggered off.

The next day, I, along with Private William Rubans, was assigned to precede the General's inspection party. We were to make sure every cigarette butt and scrap of paper was picked up.

The General, after inspecting the troops, proceeded to lead his entourage over a prescribed course throughout the battalion area. Bobwire and I stayed well ahead of the group and when we reached a deluxe eight-hole latrine on the inspection route, Bobwire decided to take a crap so I joined him. Bobwire was explaining how the Marine Corps of 1944 differed from the 'old' Corps of 1917. Suddenly the General popped in, having taken a shortcut, and approached unnoticed from the rear of the latrine. Bobwire and I both jumped up and stood at attention, our pants down around our ankles.

The General walked up to face Bobwire, looking at him for a moment then in a note of recognition said, "Bill, you old sonofabitch, I thought you was killed at the Canal."

"Yeah, George, the brass never gets the straight scoop."

The General dropped his pants and sat down next to Bobwire. "Damn it, Bill, I see you're buck private again. You been up and down the non-com ranks so many times you probably have to look at your sleeve to see if you're a Private or a Top Sergeant. What did ya do this time?"

"Pissed on the flagpole, George."

"Why the hell did you do that?" The General asked in a fit of laughter.

"I wanted the distinction of being the only Top Sergeant to piss on a flagpole. Besides, I was drunk."

"Bill you already have more distinction than any man in the corps, past or present. You can't get a medal for watering the flagpole."

"Yeah, I know, George, but I been known to do strange things when I've been drinking. Besides, I got to thinking, I'm the youngest buck private to enlist in the Corps, and I wanted to go out as the oldest buck private; I figured pissing on the flagpole during a full-dress parade rehearsal would get me busted down to private."

The General and Bobwire shot the breeze about the old days-some good, some not so good, while the entourage waited patiently, or maybe not so patiently, outside. From their conversation I learned that during World War 1 Bobwire had saved the General's life at Belleau Wood, when the General was a Second Lieutenant. They had served at various posts together off and on during the past twenty-some-odd years.

The next day Bobwire was wearing six stripes again.

After three months of jungle training, resting, and daydreaming, First Sergeant Rubin put us in touch with reality by lining us up and marching us to sickbay to receive shots.

"Where we goin, Sarg, San Francisco?" Meatnose Hillman asked.

"Yeah, that's where you're going. You're going to Frisco, and you're getting shots to protect you from 'clap' and 'syph.'"

"Where we really going, Sarg?" Johnson asked. "You can tell me; I won't tell these ass-holes. It'll just be between you and me."

"I have no idea where you're going, but I'm sure it'll be interesting. Just hope it's not as interesting as Tarawa or the Canal. Good luck, guys."

Chapter 11

GUAM

Part 1

At 0500 hours we rolled out, showered, shaved, packed our gear, and headed for the mess hall and maybe our last decent meal for who knew how long. Everyone knew where we were going but no one knew where we were going. Scuttlebutt had us landing on every island in the Pacific, including Japan, but no one knew our destination until the powers that be decided it was time to tell us.

Later that day it was announced over the p.a. that we were to join up with a convoy headed for Guam. Sergeant Lewis briefed us on what to expect.

"You heard what the man said. Our destination is Guam. For the uninformed, which is probably all of you, Guam is an island in the Marianas. The good news is most of the fighting is going on in the north and we will land in the south. However, we can expect to encounter remnants of enemy forces throughout the island. We will be on garrison, battle training recruits in a hostile region, and if the army can't handle the fighting in the north, we'll become combatants. Let's hope that will not be necessary. Dismissed. Enjoy the voyage."

The 'voyage,' as Sergeant Lewis had so generously put it, consisted of too many people in too small a space. That's the basic problem on a troopship, which in that case was a rusty old freighter converted to carry troops. It was an exact replica of the one that took us from

Samoa to Tarawa. It seemed the Navy had converted several such ships and kept them in reserve to haul troops from one lousy island to another lousy island. I remember the ship that took us from the East Coast through the Panama Canal to Samoa. It was a larger ship, a converted refrigerator ship we were told. It had more room to wander about but was by no means any better than the other two. We had to stand in a line five miles long for chow that wasn't a lot better than C rations and K rations. When GQ sounded we had to haul ass below deck and crawl onto our bunks, which were stacked five high. Mine was a top bunk, offering me one major advantage. If anyone got sick I was above the line of fire. The temperature there hovered between one hundred five and one hundred twenty degrees, a very uncomfortable place to hover. Once there we stayed until the all clear sounded, usually and hopefully just a short time. Overall it was an uneventful, boring, and uncomfortable trip. After a couple weeks at sea, give or take a few days, we arrived in Agana Harbor, not much the worst for wear but not unhappy to say adios or aloha or whatever you say at the end of a voyage. Several more appropriate expletives crossed my mind.

We were trucked inland a couple miles to a camp recently abandoned by the army. That was first rate compared to our digs at Tarawa. There was a combination mess tent and galley already in place, and quite a few of the tents had been rigged with wood frames and decks. O'Rielly, our new First Sergeant, set aside an area for those of us from Tarawa and other combat zones separate from the new guys. Reznik nailed one of the better tents that he, Meatnose Hillman, and I would share, along with two other guys, Carlos Diaz and a guy named LaRosa. An occupant, evidently left by the army guys, greeted us warmly. He let us know he was glad we were there by barking, running in circles, and vigorously wagging his tail.

"Just what we need," I said, "a mascot. What'll we name him? Anyone got any bright ideas?"

No one did at the moment as we were busy getting squared away in our new digs, but we did a few days later after we all had a chance to get acquainted with him, and each other.

LaRosa seemed kinda weird. He had a stare that bothered me. When I talked with him he looked toward but not actually at me. His stare seemed to be directed to a spot just over my left shoulder. It reminded me of a blind guy I talked to once. His stare was directed to the top of my head and a little to the right, which I could understand since he was blind. LaRosa wasn't blind, and his stare bothered me. He was twenty-two, and had served at Guadalcanal but not at Tarawa. He told us about some of his combat experiences. What bothered him most seemed a bit strange. In the jungle fighting while in a foxhole all night the Jap soldiers moved in close and shouted their mantra, "Maline die! Maline die!" Then they charged with fixed bayonets and the battle was on. LaRosa seemed more disturbed by the chanting than by the fighting. He was strange but seemed to be a stand-up guy.

Carlos Diaz was quiet and polite, an almost unheard of personality profile in that group of rough, profane, hard-drinking, womanizing (when available) combat-hardened, jarheads. He said he was eighteen but seemed more like sixteen. I heard he had fought with courage on Tarawa. He was a straight-arrow type and we were glad to have him on board.

When it came time to name our dog there were several suggestions put forward. Hillman suggested we call him Bozo. LaRosa thought Roscoe would be a good name. I suggested we call him Yardbird, until Hillman reminded me that Top Sergeant Ruban called his dog Yardbird.

"That was Kauai. This is Guam." I said.

"Good point," Hillman said. "What do you think we should name our dog, Reznik?"

"I ain't got no thought about it one way or another," Reznik said. "I don't care what you call him."

That was a strange attitude for Reznik to have, I remember thinking at the time, but made no comment.

Carlos spoke up. "We're going to call him Buster. I already call him that, and he seems to like it."

I noticed, and I think the others had too, that the dog had taken to Carlos a little more than to the rest of us.

Hillman said, "I think that's a hell of a name, Carlos. What do you guys think?"

We all agreed that henceforth our dog would be known as Buster.

Work parties were formed each day to dig latrines, police up the area, load or unload supplies, and in general bring everything up to Marine standards. When the order came to 'fall out and fall in,' we 'fell out' the back of the tent to avoid those work details. After Tarawa our philosophy was to do as little as possible and let the new guys do that crap. Most of us had lost the do-or-die, gung-ho spirit, and knew there was no glory in being dead. Everything else just seemed like bullshit. The officers knew we were goofing off but ignored it. They had other plans for us, as we were to learn later.

CHAPTER 12

GUAM

Part 2

Lazy Lattimore was more blatant than the rest of us. He never refused to join a work party, but he never worked. He never disrespected an officer, but never lifted a shovel. Even though he was lazy, he had fought gallantly during the Tarawa campaign. Probably for that reason and the fact that we were all going to be needed to help train green troops for combat, most of his behavior was overlooked. Reznik suggested another reason. Since we didn't have a brig the only way he could be punished was to stand him in front of a firing squad. That would probably have been a bit too harsh for his minor indiscretions.

Reznik and I learned of the plans they had for us. As qualified radar technicians we helped install the newly arrived radar, then were part of the twenty-four-hour-a-day operation. We were being bombed almost nightly as the airfield and radar were prime targets for the Japanese. On a moonlit night shortly after our arrival, we were under attack from the air as well as on the ground. I was on the scope, busy calling off the coordinates of incoming Japanese bombers. The rest of our outfit was outside the van, fighting off Jap patrols attempting to knock out our radar. It was a vicious battle, but on a small scale. I felt something jab me in my back, and thinking it was a Jap, spun around and stared into the barrel of a .45 automatic in the shaking hand of Lieutenant Smiley, the officer in charge of the radar van.

He screamed, "If anyone tries to leave this van I'll shoot the sonofabitch!"

Just then a bomb hit our antenna, knocking us off the air. I grabbed my carbine and headed for the door to go out and help battle the Japs. Huddled in a fetal position under a metal table was Lieutenant Smiley.

I said. "Come on, sir. We need to go out and help our men fight off the Japs."

He just whimpered and tightened the grip of his arms around his legs.

I screamed in his face, "Come on, you yellow bastard! Get up!"

He didn't move. I kicked him in the ribs and again yelled, "Get the fuck up and fight!"

He just wouldn't move. I kicked him a couple more times, probably breaking his ribs, then drug him outside and left him still rolled up in a ball like the worthless piece of shit he was.

I joined the firefight and helped the others drive off the remaining Japs. The stretcher-bearers picked up our dead and wounded, taking Smiley back with them. I expected to be put on the report for fracturing his body, but I guess he didn't want it known what a yellow, no-good coward he was.

I looked up First Sergeant O'Rielly a couple days later to report what had happened. He brought me up to speed on Smiley.

"Just another 'ninety day wonder' out of UCLA, where he took a course in electrical engineering," he said. "That qualified him to be in charge of the 270-D radar. They flew him out this morning."

"Flew him out to where, Sarg?"

"Beats me, Olson, probably to a stateside hospital. Most likely he'll get a Section-Eight and a Purple Heart for the broken ribs received in the heat of battle."

"The first day he came on like gang busters," I said. "letting us know who was in charge and how everything was going to be, and just acting like a genuine first-class ass-hole."

"It didn't take long for his true colors to come out, did it? As First Sergeant, I gotta work with these new officers a lot. They're taught to not only act as if they're superior to the enlisted ranks but to think and believe that way. Some of them actually do believe it, and eat that shit up."

"They're not all like that, Sarg. Have you ever heard of Lieutenant Hawkins?"

"Yes, I have. They named the airfield on Tarawa after him. I heard he got hit sixteen times but kept fighting until he dropped dead. I don't have any other background on him. Do you?"

"Yeah. He was in charge of a Scout/Sniper platoon that I trained with at Samoa," I said. "He and a small detachment, including a lieutenant by the name of Alan Leslie, were delivered to the pier at Tarawa in the dead of night, prior to the invasion. Their assignment was to wipe out as many of the machine gun emplacements on the pier as they could. Lieutenant Leslie was operating a flame thrower and Lieutenant Hawkins was firing a Browning Automatic Rifle. The rest of the guys carried carbines. Before they were all killed they were successful in eliminating all five machine guns."

"No kidding Olson, you trained as a Scout/Sniper with Hawkins?"

"Yes, I did. I'll tell you the story sometime, Sarg. The thing is, if they hadn't taken out those guns on the pier, a lot more jarheads would have been killed trying to get to the beach."

"You guys took it in the shorts big time on that landing, Olson. I'm not sorry I missed that action. Incidentally, I just learned they're gonna provide the troops with a two-bottle ration of beer per month."

"Did I hear correctly, Sarg? Did you say two bottles a month, not two bottles a day?"

"That's the way I hear it, Olson. Sorry it's not two bottles a day; it sure as hell should be"

Later that night in our tent, conversation was hot and heavy.

"Two bottles a month, is that what you said, Olson?" LaRosa asked.

"That's what the First Sergeant said. He said we'll get our first allotment in a couple days."

As expected, Reznik was the most vocal. "Two bottles a month is about as good as nothing. It takes one bottle to wet my lips and moisten my parched throat. Then I'm ready to enjoy a beer."

"If you don't want to wait a month, it looks like you'll have to figure out something else, buddy," I said.

Chapter 13

GUAM

Part 3

After our radar was knocked out there were seventeen of us with nothing to do until the replacement parts arrived from the States and the antenna could be repaired. Four of the guys had to stick with the radar and the rest of us were temporarily assigned to various units. I was assigned to a 155 MM howitzer. The Gunnery Sergeant decided I would be more useful as an artillery spotter since I had sniper training and was familiar with plotting map coordinates. The job of an artillery spotter was to get out in front and determine where to aim the shells so they would land on target. That's a spooky job because you're much closer to the enemy, but since that was just training I was glad to do it. It took me off the job of humping those heavy 155 shells.

From the temporary assignment on the gun crew I became part of the training program to help train newly arrived recruits. The island had been declared secure, but unlike Tarawa many Japanese soldiers remained, though not as organized fighting units. Some had escaped into the hills, never to be seen again, while others hid throughout the island, conducting hit-and-run raids. That's where we came in. The training exercises, we learned, had two objectives. One was for the new troops to get on-the-job training. The other was to eliminate the remaining Japanese soldiers who chose not to surrender. The experienced troops were to take fifty or sixty new recruits to various parts of the island, where they bivouacked under combat conditions. The hostile enemy added reality, designed to give the new guys a taste of what they could look forward to somewhere beyond Guam. The training patrols could be three to nine days' duration. The column traveled in single file, ten to fifteen feet apart, with the experienced veterans dispersed throughout the column and always in the critical position in front as 'point' and at the end as 'tail gunner.'

The patrols were long and tedious in a very hot and humid tropical jungle, with the constant element of danger. Seldom, if ever, did we complete a daylong trek without an encounter with the enemy. That, of course, was the goal, but the terms of combat seemed always to be dictated by the hunted. The column, being in the open, was easily attacked by a well-concealed enemy.

On my third patrol I got more then I bargained for. I was in the unenviable position of tail gunner and was very nervous about that assignment as it was the most dangerous place to be. About two hours into our trek the column passed an outcropping of rocks that had all the signs of a place I could expect to be attacked. I immediately went into defense mode, aiming my carbine toward the rocks as I passed by, expecting to be confronted by one or two Japanese soldiers. All my instincts told me this was going to happen. I could feel it; and my instincts were correct. I was attacked, not from where I expected but rather from above. A Jap soldier dropped on me from the branch of a tree above the trail, knocking my weapon from my hands and sending us both sprawling. He lost his weapon, a bayonet he had detached from his rifle, which he no doubt had intended to use on me. The initial advantage was his as we ended with him on top. His superior position lasted but a few seconds as I was able to get him in a headlock and reverse our positions. Size and strength gave me the power over this much smaller man, and I knew I had no choice but to kill him. I released the death grip from around his throat as I felt his body go limp.

I retrieved my carbine and fired off a shot to stop the column. My right shoulder had taken the full force of the attack as that guy had landed feet first on me, and I was hurting big time.

"Not that it makes any difference, Olson, but how come you didn't shoot the bastard instead of breaking his neck?" Sergeant Jawouski asked as he and some others arrived on the scene

"Because he knocked my carbine out of my hand when he jumped me from up there," I said, pointing into the tree.

"I know you're hurting big-time, Olson, so I'm sending you back to camp with a two-man escort. Best of luck to you, my man."

Two of the new guys got me back to headquarters, where my injuries were treated.

The up side of the attack was that I was assigned light duty while my damaged body recovered. I had ample time to think of the past and contemplate my future as I sacked out, taking full advantage of my light-duty assignment.

I was glad I'd not been part of the battle on Guam. The terrain was similar to Guadalcanal, dense jungle with a lot of hills. I could only imagine how difficult the fighting must have been. The closer to Japan the tougher the Japanese defenses were. That thought was less then comforting as I knew the training patrols we were taking the new guys on was to prepare them for a major invasion— probably an island in the Japanese chain, maybe even Japan.

As far as I was concerned, I would have been happy to stay there on Guam for the duration. Garrison duty and living conditions were easier than at Tarawa, and it wasn't nearly as hot. The blazing, dry heat was less tolerable than the hot, humid jungle of Guam. You couldn't walk ten yards without sweating but it was still preferable to Tarawa. A huge plus was, we were able to take non-stop fresh-water showers and the chow was much better.

They were showing a movie one night when the air raid alarm sounded, the first for a couple weeks. There was a mad scramble to get to our battle stations. People were running in all directions in blackout conditions. In the confusion a jeep ran over our little dog, Buster, crushing his hindquarters. His yelping was pitiful, and as much as I hated to do it, I shot him to take him out of his misery. It still chokes me up when I think about it. For a guy who cries when Lassie stubs her toe in the movies, it lay heavy on my heart. I felt like I had lost my best friend, not just a dog. We didn't talk about it, but I think the others had similar feelings. Carlos was visibly upset, and I felt particularly sorry for him.

"I knew it," Reznik said. "I knew it would happen, and that's why I didn't want nothin to do with him. I didn't want to get attached to that dog and then lose him, like when my dog, 'Dog' got killed chasing a car."

"I agree that you're better off if you don't get attached, but it's damned hard not to. Then, when something like this happens, you're stuck with your feelings. How come you didn't train your dog to not chase cars?"

"I tried, but the little bastard wasn't trainable when it came to chasing cars. Anything else, no problem, but I could never break him from that. I guess it was one of them addiction things, like smoking cigarettes. I think he was addicted to chasing cars, and there wasn't nothn nobody could do about it."

CHAPTER 14

GUAM

Part 4

The other units were getting beer every day. We were getting screwed again, same as at Tarawa. Two bottles a month was an insult, which went a long way toward telling me what they thought of us, and I was damn pissed off about it. I was never able to understand the inequity at Tarawa, so I probably shouldn't try to understand it at Guam. I figured we needed to do something for ourselves, same as we did at Tarawa. With time on my hands and my fertile mind at work, I decided to reconnoiter the island with an eye toward finding where beer was stored.

After a couple days of nosing around, I followed a path through a patch of jungle behind our tent that led to the CB camp. Their job was to keep the airstrip operational after the Japs bombed it. They were hard at work on the strip at first light, cutting out the destroyed steel matting and hauling it away, then filling in the bomb craters and laying down new matting.

The detachment at Guam was smaller than at Tarawa, but I figured they had beer to share, though of course not willingly. I needed to run this by some of the others to see if they were up for an exploratory probe to find the CBs beer.

"A raid on the CB beer supply; is that what you're asking?" Reznik said. "Dude, you know I'm up for that."

Meatnose said, "You mean like at Tarawa? Hell yes, Olson. Just say the word."

"What the hell you guys talking about, stealing the CBs beer?" LaRosa asked. "Ain't that against regulations?"

"Against regulations? Of course it's against regulations. Regulations are made to be broke. That's why they make em, so we can break em." Reznik said. "The question is, are you willing to break a few regs to get some of the beer the CBs are hoggin?"

"Hell yes. I like the way you guys think; count me in."

"I been doing some reconnoitering," I said, "and found a path through the patch of jungle separating our camp from the CBs. It's just a little way from the path to their supply tent."

"Is beer in the supply tent? Did you see their beer?" Hillman asked.

"I didn't see the beer, but I assume it's there with all the other supplies."

"Don't assume anything," Hillman said. "My dad told me that once when I was a kid, and I always remembered it."

"Your dad was probably right, Meatnose; and we're not going to walk into their supply tent some morning soon, assuming we'll find their beer and just walk away with it. Why did your dad tell you that?"

"One time I snuck his car out for a quick spin. I loved that car; it was a 1935 Buick straight-eight. Anyway, when I got back he was sitting there on the porch smoking his pipe and acting like everything was just fine. He asked me why I took his car without asking. I said I assumed it would be OK."

"Was it?" I asked.

"I assume it wasn't, Olson, because he hauled off and knocked me on my ass. When I got up he told me to never, ever, assume anything. I always remembered that."

"What's all that bullshit got to do with finding beer?" Reznik asked. "I think we need to figure out where their fucking beer is, and go get it."

"Since you always claim to be the idea man, why don't you come up with a way to do that?" Hillman asked.

"I'm glad you suggested that, Meatnose, and I'm glad you remembered it was always me that came up with the ideas. You remember on Tarawa it was my idea to steal the CBs beer? Olson and Bost planned it out, but it was my idea."

"So how we gonna find out if beer is in their supply tent?" LaRosa asked.

"That comes under the heading of planning, not ideas. But I can handle that too. Here's what we do. We slip over some night late and get real close to the supply tent and lay low for a couple hours to see if they got security posted. If we don't see anyone standing guard we slip in and look for their beer. If they have guards posted, we back out and figure another way to get their beer. How's that for a plan?"

Rezniks plan was a good one, and I was gratified to learn he wasn't a complete idiot. We waited a couple days for a full moon, then Hillman and I slipped over and hid out near the CB supply tent. We laid low for about an hour and decided there was no security, so we went in. It didn't take long for us to locate two pallets of Schlitz.

Hillman whispered, "Why not grab a case each while we're here?"

"I don't think so; I'm pretty sure I heard something. We need to slip outa' here, pronto."

That night after chow we told the others about our visit to the CB warehouse and the two pallets of Schlitz.

"All we gotta do now is work out the logistics," Reznik said. "What we'll do is, we'll slip over late tonight. I figure about two thirty or three. We'll need three guys, two to carry a case each, and one armed guard in case we run into trouble."

"What kind of trouble, Reznik?" LaRosa asked.

"Any kind of trouble. I don't know what kind of trouble we might run into. We just need to be able to handle any trouble we might run into in case we run into any trouble."

"Do you think we might run into any difficulty, Reznik?" Hillman asked. "Do you know something we don't know?"

"I don't know nothn for sure, Meatnose. I heard some scuttlebutt; but you know how scuttlebutt is. Sometime it's true but most of the time it's just scuttlebutt."

"What did you hear? We need to know what we're getting into," Hillman insisted.

"Yeah, you're right; but remember, it's just scuttlebutt. I for one think we oughta just ignore it and go ahead with our plans and see what happens."

"Knock off the bullshit and tell us what you know."

"OK, OK, don't get your bowels in an uproar, Meatnose. What I heard was, some other guys that knew about our CB beer caper at Tarawa raided the CBs beer here, and I heard there was some shots fired."

"Oh, just a few shots fired, and you weren't going to say nothn and just let us wander in there and get our asses shot off? What kinda crap is that, Reznik?" Hillman angrily demanded.

"Well, shit, Meatnose you been shot at before and lived through it. Besides, most of the time the shots miss anyway. Why do you think I suggested we go in with an armed guard? I want us to be able to cover our asses in case we have a problem."

"Do you know anything you haven't told us?" I asked.

"The story I got, but I don't know if it's true or not because it's just scuttlebutt, and you know how scuttlebutt is. It might be true and it might not be true. You never know"

"Stop the bullshit Reznik and get to the point. Do you know anything else that you haven't told us about?" I asked again.

"No…well just a couple things. The CBs got some of our guys to guard their fucking beer; some of the new guys we been taking out on training patrols. And the funny thing was, at least according to my scuttlebutt source, they didn't bluff out like they should have."

"I guess that ties it then. What do you guys want to do?' I asked.

"I, for one, don't want to get into a pissing match with other Marines, particularly if the pissing match includes shooting 'em ." LaRosa said.

"What do you want to do, Carlos?" I asked.

"I don't want to do nothing. I don't drink beer anyway; but if they had some pogie-bait or something like that I wouldn't mind stealing it, but not if I had to shoot somebody to get it, specially other Marines."

"How about you, Reznik; do you still want to go in and get their beer?"

"Hell yes. I say let's go get their fucking beer, and if them candy-ass boots try to stop us that'll have to be their problem. I know shit they never heard of and I ain't afraid to use it. How about you, Olson; you gonna wimp out on me?"

He was right about one thing. I knew he would want to do it no matter how many Marines they had guarding their beer. I also knew he wouldn't back down even if he had to take a couple of them out. I knew where to draw the line, but with Reznik there seemed never to be a line.

"Yeah, I'm gonna wimp out on you," I answered, "and it looks like the others aren't up to a shooting match with other Marines either. If you want to steal their beer, it looks like you're on your own."

Reznik stormed out, but not without telling us what a bunch of lily-livered, gutless wonders he thought we were.

That was the end of that, but I had other irons in the fire and figured we could revisit the beer issue later if the opportunity presented itself. I had been thinking about how Joe Glutz had distilled prunes into moonshine on Tarawa and wondered if we could do something along those lines. Maybe we could ferment prunes into wine.

CHAPTER 15
GUAM

Part 5

I visited the galley and got acquainted with Arnett, one of the cooks. I asked him if we could get together and try to make some prune wine. He liked the idea and said he could provide us with all the cooked prunes we needed. One of the bakers wanted in on the deal and said he could provide the yeast, which we would need if we were going to make wine.

I looked up my old buddy, Crazy Herb Johnson, from the motor pool, and told him about the plan.

"What can I do to help, Olson? I'm up for anything, even if it's something that won't work."

"That's great, Johnson. What we need is a fairly large container for a fermenting vat. I figure a fifty-gallon gasoline drum with the top knocked off and cleaned out. Do you think you can handle that?"

"Hell yes, I can handle that. When do you want it?"

"Would yesterday be too soon?"

We set it up in the jungle about fifty yards from camp and dumped in the prunes, yeast, and water. All we had to do then was wait for it to ferment. We visited our winery every day, but since our collective knowledge about wine making added up to a big fat zero, we had no idea how long to leave it. We made a SWAG calculation (scientific wild-ass guess), and figured two weeks should be enough time.

When the two weeks were up all the guys in on the deal, and a few who weren't, including some of the cooks and bakers, slipped out to the winery after chow for the official wine-tasting ceremony, a quiet and dignified affair. We dipped our canteen cups past the goop on top and filled them with what we thought would be the 'nectar of the gods.' We stood in a circle in reverent anticipation, and when everyone was ready we raised our cups while Reznik proposed a toast.

"Here's to Tojo, the sonofabitch, may his balls rot off with the seven-year itch."

We tipped our cups and took a good, healthy swig. The next instant everyone was spitting, gagging, and cursing.

"This is the most horrible goddamn crap I ever tasted," Hillman said.

Reznik agreed, adding, "You know if someone had told me it was gasoline wine and that's how it was supposed to taste I probably would have liked it."

Back in our tent, we discussed what had gone wrong. We all agreed it tasted like gasoline, with a strong metallic taste, and overall was just plain terrible.

"If that's all that's wrong with it," I said, "We should get a different fermentation vat. Glutz used lis—"

Reznik interrupted, saying, "I got an idea, Olson. I think what we oughta do is, I think we oughta midnight-requisition some lister bags from the CBs. I think we could make some good wine if we did that. What do you guys think of that idea?"

"Yeah, Reznik, I think that's a hell of an idea. I wish I'd thought of that," I said.

"I been tellin ya, I'm the idea man. Now you guys can work out the details. I gotta get some sack time before I go on watch."

Hillman said, "OK, Reznik, we'll go to work on that right away, and if we come up with something we can't handle, can we wake you up?"

"Up yours, Meatnose."

We put our midnight supply team to work, and the next day were back in business filling our new fermenting vat with cooked prunes, yeast, and water. One of the cooks thought a little sugar might help, so he dumped in about ten pounds.

Two weeks later we figured it was 'ripe' and gathered around for the big moment. Another toast to "Happier days on Guam," as we tilted our canteen cups. Our wine was definitely drinkable, and we all agreed it was great stuff, though it didn't taste like any wine I had ever tasted before.

We kept dipping our cups into the lister bag, and after a while the effects became quite gratifying. It wasn't such a bad war after all. Matter of fact, it was time to stir up some action. Crazy Herb suggested we swipe a truck and head north into the boondocks and hunt Japs. Everyone agreed that was a hell of an idea. The plan was: Crazy Herb would steal the truck, and the rest of us would get our rifles and ammo and meet Crazy outside the company area. We all filled up a couple canteens with wine and quietly slipped into camp for our gear. A few minutes later we were happily bouncing along a jungle trail not quite wide enough for a truck, driven by a crazy, wiped out driver. We didn't make much headway because Crazy kept driving off the trail and hitting trees.

About an hour later, Abe, one of the cooks, shouted for Crazy to stop the truck. I figured he had spotted some Japs, but he had a problem more urgent, than Japs as he made a dash for the bushes. We no sooner got started when someone else had the same urgent problem. As long as we were stopped I decided to solve my problem along with a couple other guys. The epidemic of GIs was upon us and we never did get all the guys back into the truck at the same time. Besides, Crazy couldn't walk straight, much less drive straight, so we stayed put. Some of the guy's were sleeping it off when they weren't going to or coming from the bushes. The rest of us were still enjoying the last of our wine. Someone suggested we were in a good spot to be ambushed since we were in Jap country and the way we had been whooping it up it was no secret we were there. We agreed we should put out a security watch, but no one did anything about it.

I woke up as the first rays of daylight filtered through the trees. I could hardly make out the details, but there were bodies sprawled all over the area. I thought all the guys were dead so I begin checking myself for blood, bullet holes or knife wounds. Nothing wrong except a brain-twisting hangover.

One by one the guys woke up, and I don't think I've ever seen a sadder-looking bunch of jarheads. As the hung-over drunks got to their feet and crawled aboard the truck we realized prune wine fresh from the vat was hardly fit for consumption unless a person needed a very powerful laxative.

Crazy was driving worse than the night before, and the jolting and bumping into trees didn't help our upset stomachs and throbbing heads. I had never been in such bad shape, and when we got back to camp all I wanted was to sack out for a couple days. That wasn't going to happen. We were greeted by no less than our company commander, Captain Clyde. It didn't take a clear head to figure out that he was pissed off big time.

First Sergeant O'Rielly bellowed, "Fall in, on the double!"

We scrambled off the truck and lined up at attention. The kindly captain proceeded to ass-chew us for about ten minutes. I recall hearing things like, 'deserters in a war zone,' and 'courts-martial,' and 'shot.' Shot? Could that be? Naw, just scare tactics, I figured. Anyway, all I wanted was for him to finish up the ass-chewing session and shut up so I could hit the sack and sleep off my god-awful hangover, but he had other plans.

"You have exactly ten minutes to draw ammunition and rations for a three-day training patrol. Now fall out and get cracking. Be back here in exactly ten minutes, or else."

It was an all-out effort as we scrambled around our tents to get ready. I had to fill my canteens, this time with water, pick up nine K rations and ammunition, pack my knapsack, haversack, and bedroll. For those ten minutes I almost forgot about the sorry condition I was in.

The green horns were lined up and ready to go when we got to the formation. The captain was looking at his watch and gave us all a fresh blast of verbal abuse as we got in line.

"Olson, take the point!" Sergeant Lewis shouted.

"Right face! Route step! Forward, march!" He bellowed, and off we went into the jungle.

"What direction?"

"Straight ahead until I tell you different."

Straight ahead was a tangle of jungle without a trail. In my weakened condition I had to chop my way through with a machete. After a couple miles of that I was exhausted. *To hell with this,* I thought. I stopped and raised my hand to signal Japs ahead.

Lewis crawled up next to me and asked, "Where are they?"

"Over to the left, about twenty-five yards," I lied.

He scanned the area and said, "I don't see nothing. You're all fogged up from last night. Fall in at the rear of the column."

"Leseberg, get up here and take the point."

I was glad to let the whole column pass by while I rested before taking up my position ten yards behind the last man. I must say, however, that I wasn't happy about my new assignment. Two weeks before, Simpson was killed while bringing up the rear, and I had no trouble remembering the guy jumping out of the tree on me. Several others had been attacked while in the position of tail gunner, though Simpson was the only one killed so far.

I remember telling myself the odds were in my favor against a repeat performance of the tree incident, but was by no means comforted by that thought and intended to do everything possible to prevent it. My head swiveled from right, to left, to the rear, and particularly toward the tree branches above as I moved forward behind the column.

Sometime later I felt a pressing urge. The prune wine was still having its effect on me and I needed to stop immediately. When I got underway a few minutes later my urgent need was to catch up to the column. That was not a good time or place to be alone, and double time was difficult with a full pack and a hangover. What I should have done and I thought of it too late was, I should have fired off a round to stop the column.

It was too late. A Japanese soldier jumped in front of me. In that instant I was gripped with terror; my heart pounded violently, and I felt weak and helpless. It was as though I was incapable of reacting to that deadly situation. I knew what I had to do, but my body would not or could not follow through. As if in a slow-motion dream I saw the butt of his rifle coming toward my head. Then my body came to life and in that split second I managed to lurch to my left, avoiding what would probably have been a deathblow. Instead of striking my head, his rifle connected with my right shoulder, knocking me to the ground. He lunged at me with the bayonet end of his rifle. The blade tore through my fatigue jacket, contacting but not penetrating my rib cage. As he withdrew his weapon I was able to grab the fore-stock of his rifle and was pulled up to my knees. As I was being pulled up he was being pulled down. There we were, face to face, both on our knees. I was bigger and stronger than he, which tilted the balance of power in my favor, and I had every intention of keeping it that way. I drew my field knife, and as he was attempting to get up, drove it toward his face and with more luck than skill plunged it into his eye. He screamed and both hands went to his face. For all intent and purposes that ended the battle. I retrieved my carbine and put him out of his misery with a shot to his head.

This skirmish wasn't over yet. Another Japanese soldier charged toward me with fixed bayonet. I leveled my carbine in his direction and put three slugs into his body. He could easily have killed me if he had shot while I was dealing with his partner, but fortunately for me, unfortunately for him, he was either out of ammunition or his weapon misfired.

Having heard the shots, Sergeant Lewis arrived shortly, out of breath and panting from his run back to my location.

"What the hell's going on?" He shouted.

I didn't think the scene needed explanation, but a dumb question deserves a dumb answer.

"Me and these guys had a disagreement, so I settled it my way. Any problem with that, Sarg?"

Lewis sent me back to camp with a two-man escort. When I got to sickbay the corpsman gave me a shot of morphine for the pain, bandaged my bruised ribs and put my arm in a sling. Later that night

I went back for another shot because I was hurting all over. Besides, I liked the way that stuff made me feel.

The next day after morning chow, First Sergeant O'Rielly stopped in for a visit. "How ya feeling Olson?"

"Sore as hell, Sarg. I'm heading over to sick bay pretty soon and try to get the corpsman to give me another shot of morphine. That's really good shit; it makes the pain go away and puts me on cloud nine. I got two shots yesterday. I'll see how many I can get today. You oughta try it sometime, Sarg, you might like it."

"Yeah, I know, Olson. I had an occasion to experience it a couple times at the Canal."

"What happened, Sarg, get shot in the ass?"

"Worse than that. Me and two other guys had to hide out for two days when the Japs overran our lines, and I had a slug in my leg."

"Sounds like you had some bad shit. How'd you get out?"

"We stayed in our foxhole covered up with tulle grass until our guys retook the area, two days later. Anyway, Olson, what I need to find out is what happened with that AWOL shit. We got a new platoon leader and he's gonna throw the fucking book at you guys."

I told him what happened when we were drunk and took off into Jap country, and what happened on patrol. I didn't lie very much about it because I knew whose side he was on. Besides, I didn't much give a shit one way or another, what Lieutenant ass-hole was going to throw at us. What could he do? Shoot us?

When O'Rielly left, I went over to sickbay and got a shot of morphine. Back in my sack I thought about our prune wine fermenting in the jungle. I didn't want to give up on it, though I didn't intend to drink any more of it in it's present form. I needed to come up with an idea to counteract the effects of the prunes, but nothing made sense. I even considered eating cheese sandwiches while drinking the wine but the longer I thought about that idea the dumber it sounded. Besides, I didn't think there was any cheese on Guam. Then like a flash I had it. We should distill our wine and try to make prune brandy.

That was such an exciting idea I almost forgot how painful my shoulder and ribs were. I couldn't wait for the guys to get back from patrol to tell them. In the meantime I needed to get together with some others and explore the possibilities of distilling our fermenting prunes. First off I needed to find someone who knew how to make moonshine. I thought about Joe Glutz and wondered if there was anyone like him in our company. I didn't think being stupid was necessary, but it probably wouldn't hurt either.

Later that day I went to the galley figuring that would be a likely place to start my search. I found Arnett the cook, who had supplied the prunes for our wine. He was stirring a big pot of what we were going to eat that night.

"Gota minute, Dude?"

He peeked into the pot, probably figuring it could do without him for a minute, and said, "Sure, Olson, what's up?"

We stepped out of the steam room tent he called a galley. As he wiped his dripping face, I told him what I had in mind and asked if he knew anyone skilled in the fine art of making moonshine.

"I heard what happened to you on patrol, Olson. How ya feeling?"

"I feel great, Arnett, and as long as they don't run out of morphine I think I'll probably be OK. Do you know anyone who knows anything about making moonshine?"

"Baker, the baker. He's a hillbilly from Tennessee. Ain't that funny, Olson? He's a baker, and his name's Baker. That would be like my name being Cook; then I would be Cook, the cook. I think that would be funny as hell. Maybe I oughta change my name to Cook. You think I oughta do that, Olson?"

"Yeah, Arnett, I think that's a hell of an idea. Do you plan on being a cook when the war's over?"

"Hell no. I hate cooking. I'm gonna help my dad run his plumbing business. The name of his business is ARNETT PLUMBING. When I get back home we're going to change the name to ARNETT & SON PLUMBING. When my kid brother, Lionel, grows up, we'll teach him how to be a plumber. Then we can change the name of our company to ARNETT & SONS PLUMBING. Then when my dad retires or dies of old age, Lionel and I can change the name to ARNETT BROS. PLUMBING. If I get married and have a son, we can change the name to—"

"That's great, Arnett," I said, interrupting any further name-changing conversation. "Can you bring Baker the baker over to my tent tonight so we can work out the details to make prune brandy?"

"Yeah, I think so. I gotta get back to work. See ya' later."

"What kinda shit ya' cooking in there, Arnett?"

"Your gonna like this Olson, It's gonna be a surprise."

"No shit, Arnett, what are you cooking?"

"No shit, Olson, it's really gonna be a surprise. I still haven't figured out what it is."

As it turned out, what he was cooking was mutton stew. He put some C rations and cold-storage onions and potatoes in, and a lot of boiled mutton from New Zealand and some canned tomatoes. Surprisingly, it was pretty damn good.

Later that night Cook the cook brought Baker the baker over to my tent.

"Olson, this here is Baker the baker," Arnett said. "We call him Clem 'cause his name is Clement. Clem, this here's Olson. He wants to turn that prune crap into brandy."

"Hi, Olson, you planning on making some moonshine?" He asked.

"Yes, I am, Clem. I want to make brandy out of our prune wine, but I don't know how to do it."

"I don't know, Olson. Arnett gave me some of that prune crap and it went through me like a dose of salts. I still ain't got over it. Just this morning, when I needed to get six loaves of bread out of the oven, I had to leave 'em in and let 'em burn because I had to run like a sonofabitch to the latrine."

"Yeah, I know, Clem, we all had that same problem, some worse than others. That's why we want to distill it into prune brandy."

"You damn sure need to do something with it. I been trying to figure out how to get it into the officers mess, but I ain't come up with nothn' yet. You got any suggestions?"

"No, but that's a hell of an idea. If I come up with something I'll let you know. Arnett told me you used to make moonshine back home. Do you think you could show us how to do it?"

"I suppose I could teach you how. I been helping my daddy and my uncle Bobby Joe and two older brothers make moonshine since I was a little kid. Most of the time we made it out of corn but when we didn't have corn we used other stuff like mash or oats. I don't see no reason why you couldn't make moonshine out of that prune crap."

"Yeah, but do you know what equipment we'd need to set up a distillery. Also, would you know how to set one up?"

"Hell yes, Olson, it's not hard. We had to set ours up all the time because the laws used to sneak in and tear it up. Then we had to put it all back together again. One time, Sammy Bob, that's my big brother; his real name is Samuel Robert, but we always called him Sammy Bob or Sam Bob. Anyways, one time a law snuck up and was gonna tear up our still and Sam Bob shot his ass full of buckshot and—"

I interrupted him and asked again if he knew what equipment we needed and if he knew how to set it up. He had all the answers, but I had a bastard of a time keeping him on track because every time he started talking it would remind him of an experience and he would launch into a long-winded story which I had no interest in. Even with all the interruptions, I was able to get a pretty accurate picture of the equipment we needed.

CHAPTER 16

GUAM

Part 6

When the training patrol returned we were in for a big surprise. All the instructors in our platoon, including me even with my injuries, were ordered to fall in on the double. None of the guys had a chance to shower and change clothes. They were dog-assed tired and hungry, but an order is an order.

We received a maximum velocity ass-chewing from our new platoon leader, Second Lieutenant, Benjamin J. Bernstein, USMCR, newly arrived 'ninety-day wonder.'

"I can and I will charge you all with being drunk and disorderly," he said, "absent without leave, and stealing government property. Those are the violations that immediately come to mind, but I guarantee there will be more when I finish my investigation. I intend to have you all stand for courts-martial, thrown in the brig, busted in rank, and restricted to the base. I'm going to throw the goddamn book at you."

"What have you to say for yourself, Private Johnson?"

"Not a goddamn thing, lieutenant. All that bullshit you just spouted don't rattle my cage a fucking bit. Court-martial don't mean shit to me. That's just another ass-chewing, and I already had a bunch of them and they ain't hurt me yet. Thrown in the brig? We ain't got a brig; didn't you know that, lieutenant? Busted in rank? Is that what you just said? Lieutenant, you need to understand something: I'm a buck-ass private. No matter how you slice it, you can't get me down no lower than that. Last week, when I was all the way up to Private First Class, the C.O. chewed my ass and busted me back down to private again because I wouldn't dig a fucking latrine. Restricted to base? Hell, that's the best place on this fucking island, and if I was restricted to base I would understand that to mean that I wouldn't have to go out on these fucking patrols, trying to teach these fucking recruits how to stay alive. That would be fine with me. However, if you told me I was gonna stand in front of a firing squad, that would be a different story. *THAT* would rattle my cage."

Bernstein stared at Crazy for a full minute with a look of complete bewilderment and consternation on his face, saying nothing in response to Johnson's tirade. Crazy had lived up to his name, and had maintained his reputation. Turning to me, the lieutenant said, "Corporal Olson what do you have to say about these violations, and what part did you play in this outrageous behavior?"

"Sir, you're pissing into the wind. Johnson pretty much just said it all. How come we get two bottles of beer a month and everyone else on the island gets two bottles a day. Why do you suppose that is, sir? Does that sound like fair and equal treatment to you? What do you suppose happened to the beer we're supposed to get? Did our beer ration find its way into the officers' mess, sir?"

"Corporal, this issue has nothing to do with beer. I asked you a direct question, which you have chosen to ignore, so I will ask again. Were you in any way responsible for this shocking disregard of regulations?"

"Sir, I have been as responsible as any of these jarheads, probably more than most, but why do you disregard my question about our beer ration? Getting fucked out of our beer ration goes to the heart of our repulsive behavior."

"Corporal, are you insinuating that the officers are stealing beer that rightly should go to the enlisted ranks?"

"Lieutenant, I ain't insinuating a fucking thing. I'm flat asking if our beer ration found its way into the officers' mess. Did it?"

The greenhorn lieutenant turned away without answering my question and went down the line, questioning everyone, receiving similar, if not more outspoken comments from each person. He couldn't understand our attitude. Stateside, his rank accorded him the respect of a minor god, but out here in the war zone he was barely tolerated. He had every intention of righting that wrong.

"You men are dismissed." Lieutenant Bernstein ordered with as much authority as he could muster. "Consider yourselves prisoners at large."

CHAPTER 17

GUAM

Part 7

"First Sergeant O'Rielly, draw up the necessary papers. I'm going to bring charges, and hold these men over for summary courts-martial."

"Aye aye, sir, I'll get on that post haste, but first can I have a word with you alone?"

"Sergeant, what did you wish to speak to me about?"

"Sir, are you completely familiar with the background of this case?"

"Sergeant, I'm as familiar with the facts in this case as I need to be. I know the laws they've broken, and I know my case is indisputable and that I'll have no problem whatsoever supporting my assertions against them. I've heard of your reputation as a 'guard house lawyer' and I suppose you'll be going to bat for these scofflaws in the upcoming courts-martial, which I fully intend to pursue. However, if there's something you think I should be made aware of, as you know, I'm duty-bound to hear you out; by all means, please do go forth with your comments."

"Can I then conclude that our conversation here will be on a 'man-to-man' basis and that I will be allowed to speak off the record, with complete and unprejudiced immunity?"

"I see no reason for not allowing you to comment on a man-to-man basis."

"Going forward then, sir. These jarheads have been in this God-forsaken part of the world for almost two years, and have survived some of the most horrendous combat imaginable. If you had accompanied them at Tarawa or Guadalcanal, which you didn't, you'd know what I'm talking about, but since you didn't, you'll have to take my word when I say it doesn't get any worse than that. History will bear me out, I guarantee. They have more than fulfilled their obligation to God, Country, and the Corps, and have been let down big time. Two bottles a month is only slightly better than no beer, particularly in view of the fact that the others who just amble in when the shooting stops are receiving two bottles each and every day. It's not disrespect or that they don't give a damn. I guess the best way to describe them is to say that they've seen the light. That is to say, they've seen too many of their buddies die. They didn't expect to still be alive, and don't expect to live a hell of a lot longer. They know anything you do to them is easy duty compared to what they've been through and what's probably yet to come. That's why they take advantage of any opportunity for diversion and mind-numbing pleasure that comes their way, to hell with the consequences."

"Sergeant, how can they consider all the violations they're charged with as being even remotely enjoyable?"

"Sir, ninety percent of the time they're thinking about, talking about and wanting just two things-women and booze. They know there isn't a damned thing they can do about women on Guam since there are none at this end of the island. Booze can be a different matter. They've been screwed out of their promised ration of beer. Why do you suppose that is, sir? It's my understanding, and I can recite facts to bear this out; the officer's mess has beer out the gazoo. I'm sure it's on the up-and-up and has nothing to do with the fact that the grunts don't get squat, but you should be able to understand why outrage and bitterness might prevail. This all leads up to the 'midnight requisition' of beer from the CBs, known as 'The CB Beer Caper.'"

"Excuse me, Sergeant, what's a seabeecaper- some kind of a fish?"

"Sir...no... it's not a *fish*. It's an incident. I know this happened prior to your arrival to the war zone here on Guam, so, before you get a skewed version of the incident, let me explain the facts."

"Sergeant, I don't want you to dump a lot of crap on me designed to divert my attention to issues that have nothing to do with the charges against these men."

"I would't do that. Please bear with me, sir. I know you want to get all the facts straight on the 'prune wine' caper, and I'll get to that post-haste. First let me fill you in on the 'CB beer caper' so you can see how it all ties in together. The Army gets beer, the Navy gets beer, the Air Corps gets beer, and the CBs get more beer than anyone. The Marines? The Marines get promises but virtually no beer. Why do you suppose that is, lieutenant? And I ask that not as a rhetorical question, but rather one that begs an answer."

"I'm sure I don't know. As a matter of fact, I don't know if what you're telling me are the true facts of the matter. Perhaps that's an issue I might pursue, after of course I have justly dealt with this current issue."

"Well, then, perhaps you and I might find common ground, so to speak, and work together to resolve that most important issue. In any event, back to the search for truth and justice in the current issue, as you put it."

"These men proceeded to midnight-requisition beer from the CBs. They'd gained some experience on Tarawa which I'd heard about but wasn't personally there."

"Excuse me, Sergeant, what do you mean by, 'midnight beer requisition'? If they have a requisition for beer, why do they wait until midnight to fill it? Before you answer I have a related question. You just told me the troops aren't getting a beer ration. If that's true, how can they have a requisition for beer?"

"Sir ... there's a great deal of difference between a beer *ration* and a midnight beer *requisition*. Bear with me and as my story unfolds and I'm sure it'll all clear up for you. Their program here on Guam was roughly patterned after the highly successful beer requisition program at Tarawa and was going along OK until the smart-ass CBs bribed some gung-ho MP types to guard their beer."

"Excuse me, Sergeant O'Rielly. Are you telling me that a beer requisition at midnight is actually an illegal raid on the CB beer supply, and that the CBs made some kind of arrangement with other Marines to protect their beer from these Marines?"

"Sir ... yes. That's precisely what I'm trying to tell you. I believe in all honesty you're entitled to know all the facts since the power to mete out justice in this very serious matter, so to speak, is in your hands. So, to continue in that vein of honesty. The Marine guards didn't bluff out, which was surprising since they were newly arrived recruits. Experience teaches that men brought into a war zone for the first time are nervous and gun-shy and by every measurement of logic should have backed down. Some shots were exchanged so it was decided to abort the raid. They let the CBs keep their goddamn beer as it wasn't worth killing other Marines for. Charges were filed when some of this crap got back to the brass but were dropped when nothing could be proved."

"Sergeant, what you're telling me about the beer incident, and what I've been told about it, supports my decision to file charges against these miscreants, and I assure you I am going to file charges."

"And you should, sir, if you think that's the right thing to do, but allow me to continue. You really need to hear this so you don't just jump in here blind, so to speak, not knowing all the pertinent facts."

"Very well, Sergeant, but please try to be brief."

"Aye, Sir. About six weeks ago Corporal Olson got into a discussion with one of the mess cooks. The cook told Olson about all the stewed prunes that were thrown out. Stewed prunes are on the prescribed list of foods to be prepared every morning, which I'm sure you already know. What you probably don't know is that nobody ever eats them. Did you know that sir?"

Lieutenant Bernstein just stared at First Sergeant O'Rielly but made no comment.

"Well sir, it's not really important whether you know that or not, however, you do know it now. Anyway, Corporal Olson and the cook came up with the idea of making wine out of the stewed prunes. The first attempt was to knock the top off and clean out a gasoline drum for a fermentation vat. One week was as long as they wanted to wait to try it. The fermented prune juice had a strong metallic taste and smelled like gasoline. Desperate as they were, they couldn't swallow the stuff. The gasoline drum couldn't be cleaned so they had to get something that hadn't been used for anything but water. They decided to requisition a lister bag from the CBs."

"What's a lister bag, Sergeant?"

"A lister bag is a rubberized canvas bag that holds about twenty gallons. It has four spigots near the bottom and is usually suspended from a tree or supported by a tripod."

"But what's it for? Are you going to tell me it's used as a container for wine for the CBs?"

"No sir, I wasn't going to tell you that at all. It's a container for drinking water on construction sites. The midnight supply team secured a lister bag, and they were back in business. The fermenting wine smelled wonderful. This time they waited two weeks for the fermenting process to do its work before trying it. They eagerly stood around the bag, dipping their canteen cups through the goop covering the juice. It tasted great, and it didn't take long before the party was in full swing."

"Were you there, Sergeant? Were you involved in stealing the lister bag?"

"Sir…no, I wasn't there; and I wasn't involved in stealing the lister bag."

"How did you know how it smelled and how it tasted if you weren't part of it? You said it smelled wonderful, and when everyone was gathered around, it tasted great. How did you know how it smelled and tasted if you weren't there?"

"Lieutenant, I wasn't there at that time. I know how it smelled and how it tasted because I smelled it and tasted it later, after the trouble was brought to my attention. I was gathering evidence in an attempt to get to the bottom of that outrageous behavior."

"To continue, after they were about half blasted some smart-ass suggested they fill their canteens and head north and hunt Japs. That sounded like a hell of an idea so they quietly drifted back to the company area to pick up their rifles and ammo. Private Johnson, one of the motor pool mechanics, appropriated a truck and picked up the men just north of camp. They loaded up and headed out on a trail not quite wide enough for a truck. Johnson, being bombed, kept hitting trees. He said he was trying to widen the road."

"After about five miles of rough riding, one of the men, Del, shouted for Johnson to stop the truck because he had to go. The prunes were starting to take effect in more ways than one. Mac took off for the bush, followed by two other guys with the same urgent calling. Those not in the bush, were drinking more of the prune wine and getting more wiped out. There was some discussion about setting out a security watch when it got dark, but they never got around to it."

"Damn it, Sergeant, the Japs could've infiltrated and killed them all. Who was the ranking non-com?"

"There were three corporals, but in their condition no one gave a damn. Corporal Olson told me he woke up at dawn and saw bodies scattered all over the area. He checked himself for wounds, but was only suffering a hangover. When they all woke up, Johnson was elected to turn the truck around and drive back to camp. He made the trail considerably wider because he was still wiped out and was seeing double and hitting trees, but they did make it back. They were all suffering hangovers, but otherwise unharmed."

"Captain Clyde was the first to greet them when they returned, and I can tell you I've never seen anyone that angry. He ordered them to fall in and proceeded to ass-chew them, and I thought he would never stop. When he finally finished, he ordered them to fall out and draw rations for a three-day training patrol. They were to wet-nurse sixty green troops who had arrived the day before."

"Do you mean to tell me, Sergeant, that Captain Clyde sent out a bunch of hung-over drunks to give jungle combat training to Marines just arrived from the States?"

"Yes sir, that's exactly what I'm trying to tell you. The patrol formed and on its way in less than an hour after the drunks stumbled off the truck. They headed for the northern region, with Corporal Olson at point. He hacked through the hot jungle for about a mile, then suddenly gave the signal to lay low, indicating Japs ahead. Sergeant Lewis crawled up to have a look. Olson pointed out where he had seen the Japs, but Lewis, not seeing anything, thought Olson was giving him a snow job just to get a rest. Breaking trail with a machete is butt-busting, hard-ass work, even for a guy without a hangover. If you'd ever done that you'd know what I mean, but of course you've never done that so, understandingly, you can't relate. No disrespect sir, but you being green and all and knowing only what they taught you in 'ninety-day wonder' school, a lot of what I'm saying will probably just go right over your head."

"Goddamn it, Sergeant, don't you dare disrespect or talk down to me. I know a hell of a lot more than you think, so knock off that crap."

"I'm sure you do, sir, no disrespect intended. To continue: Sergeant Lewis put Olson at the tail end of the patrol, by no means an act of kindness. The last man in the column is the most vulnerable and is referred to as 'tail gunner.'

"Did you know that, Lieutenant? Did you know that the last man in a column was called 'tail gunner'?"

The lieutenant glared at the sergeant, but said nothing.

"Well, sir, then I assume you do know that the last man in the column is called 'tail gunner,' and that you also understand the danger and the responsibility of that position. I'm sure you also know, the last man in the column is the person the Japs like to attack and silently kill, than kill the next person up the line and so forth. Corporal Olson, being well aware of that fact, was less than overjoyed to receive his new assignment. It was on a previous training exercise that Corporal Olson, was clobbered big time by a Jap who jumped him while he was in the very dangerous position of tail gunner. He was looking to his left when as it turned out he should have been looking up. His attacker jumped from a tree branch, landing on Olson's back, sending him to the ground and knocking his carbine from his hands. Though dazed, Olson was still able to triumph over his adversary, killing the bastard."

"You just said the Jap soldier knocked Olson's rifle from his hands. How could he kill the Jap without his weapon?"

"With his hands, Lieutenant, he killed him with his hands."

"Now you can see, sir, why Olson was nervous about that assignment; but an order is an order, and Olson, being a good marine, wasn't one to disobey an order. Anyway, there Olson was, babysitting sixty recruits in that terribly dangerous position."

"I get your point, Sergeant," the lieutenant interrupted. "You don't need to keep driving it home. Just get on with your story and try to finish up some time today."

"Sir, I'll definitely finish today, but I want to be sure you have a complete picture of all the events so you can make the right decision judging these men."

"Just get on with it, Sergeant."

"Yes sir, getting on with it. The column proceeded with a very nervous Corporal Olson as tail gunner-nervous not only from his near disaster two months prior while in that same dangerous position but nervous because he knew the enemy was near. He saw them when he was on point, and though Sergeant Lewis couldn't see them and didn't believe him, Olson knew they were close by and would probably attack the column. If they did he knew he'd be the likely target."

"So there he was, sir, fifteen feet behind the column, his head swiveling from one side to another; looking to the front, to the rear, on the ground and most particularly up into the trees. It's an old Jap trick to let the whole patrol pass, than pick off the last man. They use a knife or bayonet hoping to kill quietly than get the next man up the line."

"OK, Sergeant, it's an interesting yarn. Are you suggesting I let these men off the hook just because Captain Clyde sent them out on patrol with hangovers?"

"No, sir. I'm not suggesting that at all. I think they should all be punished for their behavior. The hangovers weren't a problem at that point. The men had probably sweat all the booze out the first hour. The purpose of this discussion is to give you a better understanding of the men you're dealing with."

"I understand the men I'm dealing with have broken regulations, and they're going to be punished. That's all I need to know."

"Sir, that's not all you need to know. You need to understand there's more to this incident than merely bending a few regulations, which is what I'm attempting to point out to you."

"Sergeant, it appears to me you're doing a much more than adequate job of presenting your version of this outrageous behavior. I agreed to listen to your input on a man-to-man basis because I felt I could gain some understanding of the men involved and what motivated them. However, I feel I'm getting more than I bargained for; but in the name of fairness I feel obliged to hear you out, but please try to make it pithy."

"Well said, Lieutenant. To continue in a more pithy vein. The patrol was hacking its way around the side of a very rough jungle-covered mountain, temporarily leaving Olson out of their range of sight. At that time a Japanese soldier jumped from behind a huge boulder, striking Olson with his rifle butt, similar to the attack two months previously. It was a powerful and crippling blow to Olson's right shoulder, knocking him to the ground and temporarily paralyzing his right arm. The reason it didn't strike him dead on in his face, as was the intention of the Japanese soldier, was because Olson lurched to the left when he caught a glimpse of the rifle butt coming at him. His attacker then thrust the other end of his rifle, the end with the bayonet attached, toward Olson, who was on the ground, seemingly helpless."

"Now do you get that picture, sir? Can you possibly imagine yourself in the position Olson was in; on the ground, having just received a paralyzing blow like that, and looking up into the murderous eyes of a Japanese soldier about to thrust his bayonet into your body? Can you put yourself in that position and imagine the terror you would feel, knowing you were about to die an agonizing, horrible death? Well, sir, that's the position Corporal Olson was in."

"Sergeant, the predicament Olson found himself in has nothing to do with him getting drunk and breaking every single regulation in the book."

"Lieutenant, he did not break every regulation in the book. He and the others just broke some of them. By no stretch of anyone's imagination did they break every single regulation in the book! With all due respect to you and your rank, sir, I feel a gross exaggeration such as that serves no useful purpose. What I'm trying to point out to you is the fact that these men put their lives on the line every day. When they step out of line at times, you should understand it's their way of trying to cope with the life-threatening danger that has become a major part of their miserable existence."

"If you think this crap you're feeding me is going to change my mind you're dead wrong, but continue with your story and try to move it along. What happened next?"

"Sir, I'm not feeding you crap. I wouldn't do that. I've been in the corps too long to disrespect a commission such as yours. But I will, as you say, move it along."

"As the Jap lunged at Olson with fixed bayonet, Olson was able to twist away so the blade wasn't plunged into his body but instead pierced his field jacket, contacting but not penetrating his rib cage. As his attacker attempted to withdraw his bayonet, Olson was able to grab the fore-stock of the rifle, and as the Jap pulled his rifle up he inadvertently assisted Olson to his feet. As Olson was being pulled up, the Japanese soldier lost his balance and was pushed down. In that instant, Olson released his grip on the rifle and stood over his adversary, who was on his knees. Taking advantage of his position, Olson withdrew his trench knife with his left hand, because as you recall he had just received a paralyzing rifle butt blow to his right arm and shoulder. You do remember that, don't you, sir?"

"Just get on with it, Sergeant."

"Getting on with it, lieutenant. Olson grabbed his trench knife with his left hand and swung wildly in the direction of the Jap's face, stabbing him in his eye, where his knife became lodged. The soldier grabbed his face with both hands, screaming in agony. Olson retrieved his carbine and pumped a couple slugs into him, taking him, out of his misery. The sound of the shots stopped the patrol."

"What happened than, Sergeant?"

"Well sir, Corporal Olson was pretty badly banged up with a lacerated and bruised rib cage as well as the damage to his shoulder and right arm. I'm sure, even though you've never experienced anything like that yourself, and probably never will, you can appreciate the fact that he had come very, very close to suffering an agonizing, horrible death. You do recognize that fact, don't you, sir?"

"Sergeant, your sarcasm is bordering on insubordination, and I suggest you tone it down. I'm getting damn tired of it. Do you understand?"

"Yes sir I do understand what you're trying to tell me, and I'll definitely show more respect to you and to your rank, sir. Now if you'll allow me I'll finish my account."

"I think your account has gone much too far already, Sergeant, so try to finish up without further delay."

"Well then, sir, without further delay, as you put it, I'll finish up. They assigned a man to get Olson back to sick bay, and the patrol continued on for two more days, killing nine more Japanese soldiers. Two of the goof-off's were badly wounded protecting the greenhorns. One of the new guys, a fellow named Jed Dakoda, was killed because he panicked. If the old salts hadn't kept their cool and controlled the situation a hell of a lot more of the new kids would be statistics. Sir, these men are professionals. They know their job and they do it well. They work hard and they play hard. They also accept the responsibility of protecting the lives of the new guys. What they expect in return is to be treated fairly. They have *not* been treated fairly, not by anyone's standards. They depend heavily on receiving their fair, daily ration of beer."

"Damned interesting yarn, Sergeant, but it doesn't cut any slack with me. You haven't given me any reason for not throwing the book at them, though God knows you've certainly tried. If anything, this bull shit-story you've been feeding me has made me more determined to prosecute them to the fullest extent allowed."

"Lieutenant, my objective here has been to make you aware of all the facts pertaining to this incident as well as to put you in touch with the reality of what these men go through each and every day. A lot of what you were taught in 'ninety-day wonder school' should be stowed in your footlocker. That crap they taught you about being superior to the enlisted ranks because you have a bar on your shoulder is pure, unadulterated bullshit. That attitude, as well as the spit-and-polish crap you learned, has no place in war. If and when you ever serve under fire and experience what this war is all about, you'll probably look back on this incident and your attitude toward these men and realize how foolish you were. If you choose to categorize as bullshit my effort to educate you in this matter, then, wrong as it is, that's your prerogative. Have you looked at the duty roster?"

"What does the duty roster have to do with this discussion, Sergeant?"

"You're scheduled to lead a four-day combat training patrol with some of these disgusting people, starting tomorrow."

"You're dismissed, Sergeant."

"Semper Fi, lieutenant."

"What does that mean?"

"Oh, I thought you knew, sir." O'Rielly said, as he turned to leave. "That's an abbreviation, the short form, you might say, for 'Semper Fidelis,' which is the Marine Corps motto, meaning alw-"

"Godamnit, Sergeant O'Rielly, I know that. I know Semper Fidelis is the Marine Corps motto, and I know it means 'always faithful,' and I know 'Semper Fi' is an abbreviated form for Semper Fidelis. I'm sure you know damn well I know all that, and I consider this statement as well as your attitude to be disrespectful and going well beyond the line of acceptable behavior."

"I'm sorry you feel that way, Lieutenant," Sergeant O'Rielly said as he turned, again, to leave.

"Hold on a minute, Sergeant. Perhaps I should phrase my question differently. What did you intend Semper Fi to mean just now?"

"It can mean a lot of things; 'Hello,' Goodbye,' 'I got mine, how you making out?' 'Do unto others, and split.' It can mean anything you want it to mean. It all depends on the situation. In your case it means C.Y.A."

"What does C.Y.A. mean?"

"Cover your ass, Lieutenant. C.Y.A. means, cover your ass!"

CHAPTER 18

GUAM

Part 8

After Lieutenant Bernstein finished ass-chewing, and the guys had showered, got some chow, and a few hours sack time, I figured they were ready to hear about my brilliant idea of manufacturing prune brandy.

I explained my plan of distilling our prune wine into moonshine. I told them about Cook the cook and Baker the baker.

"The first thing we need to get a hold of," I explained, "is a very large kettle to cook our prune wine in. Well, actually, the first thing is more prunes— a lot more prunes, because for every fifty gallons of fermented prunes we're only going to get a couple gallons of prune brandy. So, we need more prunes, a big pot with a tight-fitting lid and a substantial amount of copper tubing. We're gonna have to get-"

"Hang on a minute, Olson. How much is a substantial amount?" Reznik asked.

"Beats me, Reznik; I've never done this before. We'll have to play it by ear, like we always do. Anyway, we need to get a thermometer and requisition another lister bag from the CBs."

"Sounds complicated, Olson." Hillman said.

"It just seems that way Meatnose. It's not as complicated as you would think. Baker the baker knows exactly how to do everything, and he wants liquor as bad as we do, so he's going to help us with the whole deal."

"How we gonna get all that crap we need, Olson?" Hillman asked.

"I think we can get a lot of it from Cook the cook and Baker the baker. I think we can get a big kettle and a pot and a thermometer from them. Maybe you can talk to Crazy about getting some copper tubing from the motor pool."

LaRosa said, "Even if it don't work, it's worth a try. You can count me in, Olson. What can I do to help?"

"You can help Reznik acquire a lister bag from the CBs. Do you think you can handle that, Reznik?" I asked.

"Hell yes I can handle it, but unless you're giving orders here, which you ain't, then I think you need to ask. Maybe a 'please' would help; it damn sure wouldn't hurt."

That guy never ceased to amaze me, but I had learned early on it was best to go along with him when he came up with something weird like that.

"You're right, Reznik. Would you please take LaRosa under your wing and show him how to steal shit from the CBs? We need a lister bag."

A few days later we had all the equipment we needed, and with Baker the baker instructing us we put everything together and fired it up. We had a bastard of a time adjusting the heat as it had to be near perfect. Another problem was cooling the copper tubing, which Baker had formed into a coil.

"We always set up our still near a crick back home to cool the coils," Baker said, "but we ain't got a crick here so we're gonna have to figure out a different cooling system."

We tried different things that didn't work and ended up wrapping the coils with wet rags. We rigged a section of an exhaust pipe from a wrecked truck, jerry-rigged it over the coils, punched very small holes in it, plugged both ends and put water in it. That created a drip system on the rags, which cooled the coils. We were all surprised when it worked.

Arnett supplied us with grapefruit juice to cut the very powerful prune brandy, if and when we were, indeed, ever able to produce anything needing to be cut. We were all confident that was just a matter of time.

"How do we know this crap won't kill us?" LaRosa asked Baker the baker. "Some Army guys got hold of some alky and drank it when I was at the Canal. I think it killed one of them and put the others in sick bay."

"This ain't gonna kill nobody. It's pure alcohol, ain't nothin been added to it that would poison it. Thing is, though, you just put a little bit in a cup with a lot of grapefruit juice and it'll make ya' drunker than you might want to be."

A couple of weeks later, Meatnose and I had just finished a midnight-to-six security watch and decided to take a quick check on our still. When we arrived at the location we were shocked and horrified. Our still was gone! The lister bags of fermented prunes, the cooking pot, the coil and cooling system—everything gone! Not a trace of anything was left. How could that be? How it could be was someone had disassembled the whole damn thing and hauled it off. We combed the area, looking for anything that might give us a clue to who had done it.

Meatnose found the answer. Electric lines had been strung in the trees, passing through where our still had been. It didn't take a lot of thought to determine that the culprits responsible for this outrage were members of the Army Engineers.

"Let's follow the wires and find our still, then kill the motherfuckers who stole it," Hillman said.

"First things first, I agree we should find our still, but I'm not sure we should kill the motherfuckers yet. Let's follow these wires and see where they lead us."

We hacked our way through the jungle, following the trail left by the Army Engineers as they ran the wires through the trees. As expected, the trail ended at an Army camp. We laid low, trying to figure what our next move should be. There were several officers moving about the camp, which gave us pause. We needed to think it out so we didn't get our asses in a sling. We decided the best thing now was to back out, confer with our compadres in camp, and look for a solution.

When the others learned of our loss, the first thought shared by all was how were we going to get our still back, and what our revenge should be. The most vocal, of course, was from Reznik who was in favor of going in and massacring them all. No surprise there. Cooler heads prevailed, not to say we didn't all agree in principle with Reznik's solution. LaRosa thought it would be a good idea if there was some way we could get them to drink the prune wine. Carlos suggested a raid on their camp as we had done to the Air Corps guys at Tarawa. I think my idea was best. Hillman and I agreed we should wait until they set up the still and produced a couple gallons of prune brandy, then go in and take the whole works back, including the brandy, of course. A little ass kicking would go a long way in the direction of revenge as well as restoring our self-image; that of being very tough hombres.

However, we weren't able to implement any of those plans as we had received orders to move out of Guam. Retribution, it seemed, was no longer an option as we would be on our way to parts unknown shortly.

"We still have a few days before we leave." Hillman said. "I got an idea how to get even with the ass-holes who stole our still."

"What do you think we oughta do, Meatnose?" Reznik asked.

"I think we need to search the area for our still, and when we find it, I think we should destroy it so those bastards can't use it."

"That's a hell of an idea, Hillman," I said. "It shouldn't be too hard to find. It's probably close but not too close to their camp, and we know where that is."

We searched the area not far from their camp and found what we were looking for. It was easier than we thought it would be, and we wasted no time rendering every part of what was at one time a labor of love into a useless pile of junk.

Justice was served and we were all satisfied with the results.

CHAPTER 19

A SLOW BOAT TO OKINAWA

Part 1

Landing Ships Tank (LST), designed with a flat bottom, enabling them to deliver armored tanks directly to the beach as part of an invasion force, and were capable of carrying as many as ten Sherman tanks. They weren't designed to carry troops, but some were converted for that purpose because of the shortage of troopships. They were fitted out with enough bunks to accommodate a platoon. Our platoon was unlucky enough to be designated as passengers on one such vessel, LST-20.

By midnight of a moonlit night in March of 1945, we were loaded aboard LST-20 along with all our gear, including everything needed to fight a war. We weren't overjoyed when told we were on our way to Okinawa and were going to be part of the invasion. There just didn't seem to be a happy place in that part of the world at that time in history.

Leaving Agana harbor was a comedy of errors. The captain was evidently new at commanding LSTs. He had recently skippered a PT boat and seemed not to appreciate that an LST lacks the agility of a PT boat. While trying to maneuver his way out of the harbor he steered us into a troopship.

A bullhorn blared at him, "Get control of your goddamn ship! Steer hard to port!"

The LST skipper shouted to his helmsman, "Full astern!"

The bullhorn shouted, "Not astern, ya' dumb bastard! Steer hard to port!"

Then the LST banged into another ship. The captain of that ship got on his bullhorn and blared out another set of instructions. "Steer hard to starboard and stay the hell away from my ship!"

Then the two bullhorns began shouting at each other, all the time raising hell with the skipper of the LST. Then another bullhorn entered the fray.

"This is Captain Hearld speaking. If you don't know how to run that goddamn ship, turn the wheel over to any seaman first and get your ass off the bridge. You're heading directly to my starboard."

Adjustments were made and the hard-luck LST finally got out of the harbor without any more collisions and we headed out to sea on our way to Okinawa. I for one had no confidence that we would ever reach our destination. With a skipper in command who seemed incapable of steering us out of the harbor the chances of reaching our destination seemed slim.

The LST by nature is a very un-seaworthy vessel by reason of its flat bottom and was the victim of the open sea. In a following sea it pitched fore and aft as well as rolling port to starboard. It was slow, moving at a top speed of eight knots, and if the wind was from our stern and was blowing over eight knots, we were unable to keep ahead of the diesel exhaust. Most of us were seasick, and the decks were awash with vomit for the first three days. When we gained our sea legs and got used to breathing diesel exhaust fumes, we settled into an uncomfortable and boring four-week journey. Life consisted of writing letters, reading, or playing acey-deucy, but the main interest and entertainment was poker. Several games were always in play and only shut down to eat and sleep. It was the center of attraction for players and non-players alike.

As the days wore on there were fewer but larger games. Late one night while enjoying a run of good luck, accumulating sizable winnings, I needed to leave the game for a quick trip to the head but never returned to the game. I was waylaid in a dark passageway and woke up with a giant headache and all my money gone. My only recollection was of being jumped from behind and hearing that person say something that sounded like, "Tellahut…" before my lights went out.

"Tellahut…" made no sense to me, but it was the only connection I had to being cold-cocked and robbed. I made my way to my bunk and crashed, thinking I would treat this hit on the head the same as a heavy drinking bout by sleeping it off. I woke up the following afternoon feeling sick and still sporting a huge headache. When I explained to Reznik what had happened he took me to sick bay where I was taken care of for the next few days. I told the corpsman I slipped and fell in the passageway.

I kept quiet about the incident, figuring nothing could be gained by telling anyone, but vowed to find my attacker and kill the sonofabitch. I didn't join any more poker games but spent many hours as an observer with but one objective, that of finding my assailant.

A week or so later another incident occurred, which served to divert my thoughts back to boot camp. I was leaning on the rail, observing the other ships in our convoy when my attention was drawn to a marine sitting on the top rail looking out to sea. His heel was hooked over the bottom rail. The reason he caught my attention was because he was painted purple, a medication for coral poisoning. As I looked at him more closely I felt I knew him but couldn't remember from where. As I edged closer to get a better look he turned toward me and in that instant I was pretty sure I knew who he was.

"Corporal Blood?" I asked.

"My name's Mathews. Sergeant J. Mathews. Who the fuck are you?"

"Olson. Corporal Dennis H. Olson; but I doubt you remember me. If you do it would be as Recruit Olson, but it doesn't matter if you remember me or not. I damn sure remember you."

With that I reached down and unhooked the heel of his boot from the bottom rail and flipped him over the side. His scream ended when he splashed into the ocean.

"Man overboard!" I yelled.

I never saw the bastard again and could never be sure if he got picked up by one of the other ships in our convoy or not, and to this day I don't care one way or the other.

Chapter 20

A SLOW BOAT TO OKINAWA

Part 2

It was my misfortune to end up in Corporal Mathews' squad for boot training at SDMRD (San Diego Marine Recruit Depot). I could just as easily have been assigned to Sergeant Wordell or Private First Class Gonsolaz. They and Corporal Mathews had all been in the Corps since before the war started and had been assigned the duties of DI (Drill Instructor) there at San Diego.

Corporal Blood was the name the members of my platoon hung on Mathews. He was the meanest, most sadistic sonofabitch I ever met before or since. Not to be confused with the general concept of the role of a DI— that of training young recruits the brutality of killing. One of his favorite disciplines, when he thought discipline was called for, and the inspiration for the name "Corporal Blood" was to order the troops down on their knees and slap the blacktop parade ground until their hands bled. While performing the manual of arms he wanted to hear a loud crack as the recruits slapped the leather rifle slings, but the sound was never loud enough to satisfy him. That was but one of many supposed infractions prompting the punishment.

The slightest breaking of a rule or error in a drill routine was all he needed to inflict that torturous discipline on an individual who didn't measure up to his expectations. Oscar Gormier was one of his favorite victims because he had a problem with a particular rifle drill.

The drill was actually not very difficult, but for Gormier it seemed to be. It was obvious to us all that Corporal Blood took pleasure in meting out his favorite punishment to Gormier and seemed to put us through that particular drill an inordinate amount of times. Gormier, didn't miss the drill every time but if put through it often enough eventually would screw up. Down on his knees he would go, slapping the tarmac until his hands bled. Dumb as he was, he figured a way to cut short the torture. He rubbed the tarmac each time he slapped his hands down, causing them to bleed, thus ending the torture sooner. If our beloved DI had actually wanted Gormier to learn that routine he could have had him do repetitions of it until he got it right without the unnecessary punishment. That's what the other DIs would have done, but that wasn't the way of Corporal Blood.

Mathews didn't appreciate the title "Corporal Blood" which had spread throughout the company and to the other DIs, who took to using that name when addressing him. He knew it had originated in our platoon, which prompted him to inflict other punishments on us. One of his favorites was to have an individual do one hundred 'up and overs' for a real or imagined error or infraction of the training manual. 'Up and overs' was a drill requiring the boot to grip his rifle, palms down, his left hand gripping the barrel and his right hand gripping the stock. He then was to push it up, extended over his head, lower it behind his head, extend it back up over his head and bring it down to its original position in front of him. Very few people were able to complete one hundred repetitions, so were made to stand at attention during evening chow until just prior to the closing of the chow hall before being released to eat.

He often called an individual into his office for rifle inspection. A microscopic particle of dust that only he could see prompted him to order one hundred 'up and overs.' When my turn for rifle inspection came up I failed, prompting Corporal Blood to order the usual punishment. After completing that drill he ordered me to extend my arms out, palms down. He then placed the rifle across the back of my hands, telling me to hold it there, or else. In about two minutes my arm muscles began to spasm, causing my rifle to bounce, then crash to the deck. When I bent to pick it up, Blood bellowed. "Stand at attention, you stupid sonofabitch!"

I snapped to attention as Corporal Blood stood nose to nose with me, screaming every expletive and insult known to mankind. His face was beet red and the blood vessels in his neck seemed ready to explode. Suddenly, seemingly unable to control his anger, he slammed his fist into my face, knocking me through the thin composition end wall of the Quonset hut. I was on my back in the company street, semi-conscious, bleeding from my mouth and nose while Blood stood over me still cursing. He bent down and screamed, "You busted my fucking wall you dumb bastard!"

I yearned for the day I might meet Corporal Blood and even the score.

Chapter 21

A SLOW BOAT TO OKINAWA

Part 3

After three weeks of plugging along at eight knots, other ships came into view and we became part of a larger convoy. The fourth week, as we neared Okinawa, things begin to liven up. Japanese planes filled the skies and were attacking the ships in our convoy, diving into them with total abandonment of their own survival. They were the last line of defense in the landing of Okinawa. They were the infamous Kamikazes. Translation: "Divine Wind." Many of them were shot down and plunged into the sea, but many others were successful in their mission of destruction. Their targets of choice were the larger warships and troopships, but most particularly our aircraft carriers. It was a spectacular show, and as we drew closer, were drawn into it.

I was assigned the task of passing drums of .50 caliber ammunition up from the ammo locker below. Halfway up the ladder, I stood on one rung and hooked my leg over a higher rung. Forty-pound drums were passed up to me, and I in turn passed them on up to the next guy. This arrangement was going fine until the guy above me got excited and dropped a drum of ammo on me. I was stripped off the ladder and fell to the deck below. In sick bay I was patched up and told I was the first casualty on LST-20 in the battle of Okinawa. That and five cents would buy me a cup of coffee back home.

The scene, as we approached the harbor defied description. It was a very large harbor and was full of all manner of vessels. When we reached our designated place on the beach, the ramp was dropped and we exited LST-20, fully expecting to meet defending Japanese forces. Much to our gratitude and relief the enemy was nowhere to be found, so we took up defensive positions, awaiting further orders.

The beach, as far as the eye could was lined with all manner of landing craft. LSTs, such as the one we were vacating, and Higgins boats by the hundreds were off-loading Marine and Army infantry combatants. Tanks, trucks, jeeps, artillery pieces, and all manner of supplies and equipment were being deposited onto the beach from barges. It was an awesome sight. As we were forming up on the beach, our attention was drawn to the sky. One of the Kamikazes was circling a DE, (Destroyer Escort), seemingly preparing to make his fatal crash dive when it was hit by .40 millimeter fire from the DE. The aircraft went out of control and headed directly toward us. Everyone scattered and hit the deck.

Luck was on our side, as it veered at the last minute, crashing into LST-20 amidships. We learned later that twenty crewmen were killed and many others injured.

If the Kamikaze had hit moments earlier, many Marines would have been casualties, but, fortunately, the only Marine casualty was Big Jake. Jake was one of the big winners in the poker games. His knapsack and haversack were packed full of money. The chaplain took charge of his winnings, promising to send the money home to his family. He probably did. He seemed an honest, straightforward sort.

I often wondered if Big Jake was altogether an honest poker player or if he might have had skills far greater than the average jarhead with but a cursory knowledge of the basics of poker but none of the intricacies of the game. I'm not saying he was anything less than a straight-arrow player, but it did strike me that his extraordinary luck was more than just somewhat questionable.

We were met by ferocious swarms of biting, blood-sucking fleas. That unexpected encounter created a great deal of discomfort for us all as we attempted to get them out of our eyes, ears, nose, and every opening of our clothes. I couldn't help thinking at the time that the reason we weren't met by enemy resistance was because the enemy didn't want to deal with those miserable insects.

CHAPTER 22

WHERE ARE THEY?

On the plus side of Okinawa was the weather. We were no longer in the dreaded tropics but rather in a temperate climate. However, issues more important than fleas and weather were on the agenda. Since the Japanese didn't meet us at the beachhead as expected, the search was on to locate their main forces. The Third Marine Division marched all the way across the island, while the First Marine Division was sent north. The 27th and 77th Army Divisions went south.

My experience as a radar technician wasn't needed at that time, so I was assigned to the 2nd AAA Battalion of the First Marine Division. My training with the Scout/Sniper unit at Samoa as well as the temporary assignment to a 155 mm howitzer as a spotter while at Guam came back to haunt me. As we advanced north we began receiving artillery rounds so were temporarily stopped until that problem could be resolved. I was one of the spotters sent ahead to zero-in on the location of the enemy, and was assigned a communications man named Delbert to take care of the field telephone. He was fresh from the States and scared shitless.

It was a very dark night as we crept to our forward position, laying a telephone line as we went. When we got to about a mile ahead of our company I spotted a disabled Jap tank. That seemed a good place to hide and try to pinpoint the enemy so we could direct artillery fire. We no sooner got covered up when a Jap soldier passed about ten yards from us, much too close for comfort, I figured. We had come closer than we should have and needed to back out as soon as possible.

As I was gathering up our gear Delbert stepped away from the tank to take a leak. My feelings went from anxiety to raw fear as a Jap soldier passed within spitting distance of me as he slipped up behind Delbert. I could see he was alone and wearing a sword, meaning he was an officer, not a soldier. I needed to kill him before he killed Delbert.

I withdrew my kabar knife and managed to slip up behind him before he reached Delbert. I grabbed his face and snapped it back, giving a sharp twist to the left, and cut his throat with one swipe of my knife. He died without a sound, and as he slid to the ground I was able to grab his sword.

It occurred to me as I backed away from his lifeless body that I wasn't bothered in the slightest at taking this man's life in this most brutal manner. Thinking back to my first victim on the beach at Tarawa and how disturbing it was to know I had taken a human life and contrasting that to my lack of feelings when I killed the Japanese officer, I concluded that I had developed into what the Corps wanted—a human killing machine. I say that not with pride nor shame, but with the knowledge that it was a reality that could not be avoided. You kill or be killed. If you're victorious in each and every one of these combat situations your reward is, you continue to live.

However, that wasn't the end of the story. I was beginning to learn that the price you pay for victory was the ghosts inside you and the effect they have and will continue to have on your life. That was something I never worried about then or even considered because I actually didn't think I'd go home. I knew that eventually I'd be killed- if not that day then surely the next. Since that wasn't my fate, and I thank God for that daily, I suppose the price I paid for my life was and is the ghastly dreams I have had to contend with all these years and how my life has been affected, even defined by them.

I told Delbert we needed to get out of there fast before they came looking for the officer I just killed. He had a dazed look and just stared at me. I think he was shocked by what he saw so I punched him in the stomach to get his attention. After he regained the ability to breath, we crawled back about one hundred yards toward our lines. I told Delbert to call for artillery fire and covered him with my poncho as he read the coordinates to the artillery gunner. It called for fire to land one hundred yards beyond the Jap tank.

We decided to lay low until the artillery fire started, then haul ass back to our lines. However, instead of the shells landing one hundred yards beyond the tank, they were landing one hundred yards short of the tank, which was where Delbert and I were hunkered down. Artillery shells were dropping all around us instead of on the Japanese lines. I told Delbert to get his phone out and abort the shelling, pronto. He corrected the coordinates and we huddled up and waited for the shelling to stop. Delbert wasn't the only one scared shitless as we carefully made our way back to the comfort and safety of our comrades.

Chapter 23

THE BATTLE

We could have continued marching north all through Okinawa and not found the main Japanese forces. The 27th and 77th Army Divisions, who had gone south, encountered the bulk of the Japanese forces, which were well armed and fortified. Fighting was fierce, with heavy losses on both sides.

The Army general, General Buckner, had a notion he could save lives by blasting the Japanese with artillery. He used his field pieces, which included 90 mm AAA and 155 mm howitzers, supported by the fourteen and sixteen inch guns of the Navy battlewagons and the smaller guns from the cruisers to accomplish this. They blazed away at the enemy with such ferocity they were burning out the barrels. The Army was still losing hundreds of their troops, killed and wounded. It became apparent that tactic wasn't working as the Japs were in key positions and well dug in. It could only be done with overwhelming forces of manpower.

More troops were needed if the battle was to be won. The High Command ordered the Marine divisions south to join the war. General Buckner was killed while visiting a forward artillery observation position. He was replaced by Marine Corps General Gieger, who took command of the Okinawa operations on the ground, and the bombardment was halted.

After trekking north in search of the Japanese forces, we re-traced our steps and headed south where the battle was taking place, and where the Army divisions were in great need of support. My company was assigned the task of attacking the southern part of the line between Shuri Castle and Naha City, the capital of Okinawa. That involved house-to-house and building-to-building street fighting. We had never been trained for that type of combat and our involvement became a very costly on-the-job learning process. As we advanced through the city we received a fierce barrage of .50 and .30 caliber machine gun fire, from guns mounted in and on the buildings. Snipers were everywhere, firing from around every corner, window, and rooftop. Our losses were heavy; members of my platoon were dropping all around me, killed or wounded. What to do? I threw grenades as fast as I could pull the pin, and fired my carbine at anything that looked like a machine gun emplacement or an enemy sniper, emptying clip after clip into windows and doorways. Others were firing mortars and bazookas. There was every indication that my pre-determined prophesy would occur in that, the most ferocious of battles to date for me, even including Tarawa. Every minute I expected to go down.

By day we fought our way into the city in this manner, but when night fell the enemy forces drove us out. We retreated to where we could dig in and defend ourselves during the night and launch another attack on the city the following day. That pattern continued for four days and four nights. Our losses were so heavy we were unable to continue our assault and were ordered to pull back to a new more defensible position where we established a battle line and dug in. Our no-win situation was a desperate one, and the expected replacements were nonexistent.

Orders came down that no one was to be taken off the line unless he was physically disabled by gunshot or shrapnel. Dengue fever didn't count. Dengue was so debilitating, those experiencing it were often too sick to move out of their foxhole to relieve themselves. Even if they had been able to exit their foxhole, they would probably have been killed by enemy fire.

My buddy Reznik and I were part of that desperate situation-sharing a two-man foxhole. I had been feeling sick for a couple days and was pretty sure I had contracted the dreaded dengue. I was desperate to get out of that stinking hole and into the field hospital for treatment, but the order to stay on the battle line prevented that.

CHAPTER 24

DESPERATION

We had been in that hole four or five days; I wasn't sure as I had lost track of time. The one thing I was very sure of was that I wouldn't live through another night. We were all in bad shape and there weren't enough of us left to repel an assault. That was truly a hopeless situation, and I desperately needed sleep and something to eat, and for those goddamn fleas and mosquitoes to quit biting me. I looked up and into the eyes of a Jap soldier on the edge of my foxhole. I stared up at him, and he just stood there looking down at me, laughing. I wondered why he didn't shoot. Then, as fast as he appeared, he was gone. I had experienced hallucinations before but that one was so realistic I thought it was actually happening. It was Reznik's turn to sleep, and my turn to stay awake and have hallucinations.

Why not wake him up and tell him he's on his own and just walk away? I could report to an officer behind the lines; tell him I wasn't feeling well and didn't want to be part of this battle anymore. I could tell him I had a real bad headache and needed an aspirin. He would probably send me to the field hospital. Now that I'm out of that foxhole I might as well be in Seattle shacked up with Linda. Damn she was sweet!

"Reznik, wake up. I got an idea how we can get out of this goddamn place. Wake the hell up. You're gonna like this idea."

"Damn it, Olson, it's not time for me to wake up yet. I'm not asleep anyway. What the fuck do you want?"

"If we shoot each other, they'll take us off the line."

"Olson, for Christ's sake, why would we want to kill each other? The Japs are trying their damndest to do that and probably will. Unless I miss my guess the next counterattack will wipe us all out."

"I don't mean kill each other, you dumb bastard. I mean just shoot each other in the arm or leg. If we're wounded we'll be taken off the line."

"That's a hell of an idea, Olson. Are you serious about it?"

"Hell yes, I'm serious. What do we have to lose? We're not going to live through another night in this hole anyway. It's probably our last chance to stay alive."

"You ain't wrong, buddy; I reached the end of my line two days ago. I'm up for anything, even something that won't work. I just don't give a shit anymore."

"So, how shall we do it?" I asked.

"Why the hell are you asking me? It's your idea, not mine."

"OK, Reznik. I knew you'd leave it up to me to figure out, so here's what we'll do. We'll draw straws to see who gets shot first."

"I don't see any straws Olson. How we gonna draw straws if there ain't no straws to draw? I think we oughta toss a coin. You got a nickel or something?"

"No, but I got this lucky coin I been carrying around since I was in high school. Come to think about it, maybe it's what's kept me alive. Anyway, it's got a naked girl on one side and a jackass on the other side. I'll flip it and you call it. When it's in the air you call out, 'naked girl', or 'jackass.' If it comes up what you called, that means you win and you shoot me first, then I shoot you. If it comes up what you didn't call, that means you lose and I shoot you first, then you shoot me. Do you understand that?"

"Yeah, that works for me, but let me see the coin first. What if it has a naked girl on both sides and no jackass? Or what if it has a jackass on both sides and no naked girl?"

"Goddamn it, Reznik, do you think I'd carry around a coin with a jackass on both sides?"

"Yeah, I guess you got a point there, but you damn sure could have a coin with a naked girl on both sides. Let me see the fucking coin."

"Sure, you can see the fucking coin, but let me ask you a question first. What the hell difference does it make if it has a naked girl on both sides or a jackass on both sides or if it has a naked girl on one side and a jackass on the other side? What the hell difference would it make? What we're trying to do here is, we're trying to decide who's gonna get shot first, right?"

"Yeah, you're right. I just don't want to get screwed on this deal like you're always trying to screw me. I remember on Guam when you changed the duty roster and I got stuck doing five training patrols in a row and you didn't do shit."

"That's because I was working on the radar antenna."

"Well, I'm supposed to be a radar tech, same as you. How come I wasn't working on the antenna?"

"The key word here is *supposed*. Anyway, I didn't change the fucking schedule. O'Rielly didn't put me back on rotation when we got the antenna fixed. He fucked up the schedule, I didn't."

"There you go, blaming O'Rielly, the best First Sergeant we ever had as far as I'm concerned. How about the time he got us off the hook when we got drunk on that prune wine shit and went AWOL?"

"Reznik, how come every time you're wrong about something, which is most of the time, and we get into an argument about it and you lose the argument, which you always do, how come you always change the subject to something else? Why do you always do that?"

"I don't want to get screwed on this deal, Olson. This is a damn big thing we're talking about doing here."

"Well, how the hell you gonna get screwed? It's simple as hell. We shoot each other and get out of this fucking battle. What else do you need to know?"

"OK, Olson, I agree. The main thing is to get out of this stinking hole, so let me see the coin so we can proceed."

"Reznik, you're the most hard-headed sonofabitch I've ever known. Here, look at the fucking coin and tell me what you see."

"OK, OK. You don't need to get your bowels in an uproar. You're right. I can see both sides. She's kinda cute, isn't she? Tell ya' what, Olson, I get the girl and you get the jackass. How's that for a deal?"

"Here's the way we should do it," I said. "I'll flip the coin and you call it in the air. If you call it right you shoot me first. Do you agree that's the way we should do it?"

"Yeah, that's the way we should do it. Go ahead, flip the coin."

I flipped the coin in the air, caught it and slapped it on the back of my other hand. He called, "Naked girl." No surprise there; I didn't think he'd call, "Jackass"

It came up jackass.

He stared at the coin, then said, "I think we should do two out of three. That would be more fair, don't you think?"

"Reznik, why don't we just forget the whole fucking thing? I don't think you want to do it anyway."

"There you go again, Olson. Every time I suggest something, you get pissed. Don't you think two out of three is more fair than one out of one?"

"OK we'll do two out of three, but if you lose again we're not gonna do three out of five. Do you agree to that?"

"Yeah I agree. Go ahead, flip it again."

He lost again, and I pulled out my .45 and jokingly asked him if he had any last request.

"Damn it, I'm nervous enough about this. No more goddamn jokes, OK?"

"OK, no more jokes. But I thought that was a pretty good one, didn't you?"

"Just shoot me and get it over with."

"OK hold your arm still"

He was shaking all over. "Hold your goddamn arm still or I'm not going to be able to do this."

"That gun makes me nervous- it looks like a 155 millimeter howitzer. What if you miss? You might hit me in the head. I might just as well stay in this fucking foxhole and take my chances here as to have you shoot my goddamn head off."

"I'm not going to shoot your goddamn head off. I won't miss if you hold your fucking arm still. I think you're chickening out."

"I'm not chickening out, I just don't want you to kill me."

"Hold still, damn it; I'm not going to kill you. This is just gonna be a flesh wound- you won't feel a thing."

"Don't give me that crap, Olson, I been shot before. Remember? I know what it feels like."

"Damn it, Reznik, if you don't want to do this, just say so."

"I want to do it; go ahead, shoot me."

I lifted up my .45 and took aim.

"No! Hold it! Wait a minute! Don't shoot!"

"Reznik, for Christ-sake, now what's your problem?"

"I don't want you to shoot me in my left arm. If I'm going to be shot in the arm, I want it to be my right arm."

"How come?"

"How come? Because I'm left-handed, why the hell do you think?'

"OK, are you ready now, or do you want to talk about it some more?"

"Yeah, I'm ready. Go ahead, Olson shoot me."

When I fired, the bullet went through Reznik's arm and broke the bone. The lower part of his forearm just hung down.

"Goddamnit, Olson, you damn near shot my whole fucking arm plumb off. Look at what you did."

At that point, Reznik passed out. I called out for a corpsman, but none showed up.

What the hell was I going to do now? Reznik was bleeding pretty bad, and I knew I had to stop it. I used an ammo bandoleer as a tourniquet wrapped around my bayonet for pressure and was able to stop the bleeding. I decided to chance getting shot by leaving the relative safety of the foxhole. I dragged Reznik a hundred yards behind the lines, all the time yelling for a corpsman. A corpsman finally showed up and gave Reznik a shot of morphine and helped me carry him to an ambulance, which transported him to a field hospital.

I made my way back to the front lines and to the dreaded foxhole without getting shot. I settled in with the mosquitoes and fleas and stench, and tried to make sense out of what had happened, but the more I thought about it the less sense it made.

Why did we think shooting each other was such a bright idea? What did we accomplish? Reznik was off the battle line, but his arm looked so bad he'll probably lose it. Hell, after seeing what I did to his arm I'm glad I didn't go first. First, hell. First was all there was. There was no second. Christ, I wish I hadn't pulled the trigger. That was a stupid idea. His arm looked terrible; I wonder if he'll lose it. I'll apologize when I see him, if I see him. Hell, I might never see the ass-hole again. Maybe he'll get shipped out to Hawaii before I get out of this hole. It wasn't all my fault. He wanted to get out of this battle as bad as I did. Semper Fi, buddy. I hope you make it. I'm back in this stinking hole, only now I'm alone and I'm sicker than hell. I'm so damn weak I don't think I could pull the trigger if I had to. I don't think I'm gonna make it out of here. This is worse than Tarawa, certainly worse than Gaum. Reznik, you're probably gonna lose your arm, but I think I'm gonna die. Damn it's cold. I don't remember it being this cold. I can't stop shaking. Shit, it's not gonna do any good to cry. What if someone sees me? Fat chance of that. I'm all alone here and I'm pretty damn sure I'm gonna die.

I would never have joined the Marine Corps if I'd known I'd end up in a stinking foxhole on Okinawa, filthy dirty and starving, feeling more dead than alive from dengue fever or malaria, or both, and lack of sleep. Those were my thoughts as I fell in and out of sleep in that most horrible of situations. My thoughts drifted back to the day I joined The Marines.

Chapter 25

BACK TO THE BEGINNING

I felt it was time to offer myself up to my country. The date was March 20, 1943 and I was in Seattle, Washington.

"You mean if I join the Navy I gotta wear one of those silly looking monkey suits?" I asked the Chief Petty Officer in the Naval Recruiting Office.

That seemed to piss him off.

"I got just the deal for you, son; follow me," he said as he led me next door to the Marine Corps Recruiting Office.

Four months later only one phase of boot camp remained. It was time for our platoon to qualify on the rifle range at Mathews.

Sitting in the bed of an open truck, Private Hillman asked, "How did ya' shoot, Olson?"

"Squeaked by as expert," I answered. "Lucky, I guess. Got a possible on the five hundred. How'd you do?"

"Sharpshooter," he replied. "Missed expert by a lousy two points. I'm glad it's over."

Thinking back to the past two weeks at the rifle range, I had looked forward to going if for no other reason than to get away from the dull, exhausting routine of close order drill and particularly from the sadistic antics of our beloved DI, Corporal Blood.

The officers and non-coms had been blowing smoke up our asses about the importance of shooting a high score. Over, and over, and over, it had been pounded into our heads. "Every Marine must qualify with a rifle."

"Getting a high score is the most important part of your training. It will influence your entire career in the Corps and enhance your sex life forever."

"The prestige of the Corps depends on your score."

"Your life and that of your fellow Marines may depend on your score and how well you shoot."

"The score you get can and will affect the outcome of the war."

"The human race lies in the balance of you getting a high score."

"Blah, blah, blah." On and on it went.

"It'll be a cold day in hell before I forget the chow at Mathews," I said.

The high level thinkers must have believed all the bullshit about how carrots benefited your eyesight because they came up with the idea that eating copious amounts of carrots would improve our shooting score, probably based on the theory that if a little does a little good a lot will do a lot of good.

"Yeah, but kee-rist," Hillman stuttered, shivering from the wet chill. "G-g-goddamn carrots three times a day. I been hungry ever since we got to the range because I couldn't eat that shit. Had a few bucks stashed that I gave to one of the mess-cooks to save me some scraps from the officers' mess."

"Be thankful, Hillman. All I had besides carrots was that goddamn chopsuey they served us, which was like eating shit with a dirty spoon."

"Yeah, that was some bad stuff, Olson. It was so bad I guess they figured we'd eat less of it and more carrots. Their thinking process is nothing short of brilliant. Chow call turned out to be fall out and draw garbage."

The weather had been clear and hot during the tiresome snapping-in period, but when the long awaited day arrived it rained. A pink-faced Second Lieutenant in starched khakis stood up in front of the platoon.

"At ease, men," he squeaked above the sound of the rain. "Today's the big day- the day we've all been preparing for. Today we'll separate the men from the boys. This is what the Corps is all about." He was so impressed with being a part of this momentous historical event it seemed he couldn't stop talking. When he finally finished his stupid blather we marched to the range where we had to listen to another longwinded speech about range safety from the Range Master.

"All ready on the right...All ready on the left...Lock and load... Commence firing."

"I'm glad it's over," Hillman said as he tried to get lower in the truck bed, "even if I didn't hit the bull at five hundred yards."

"I hit it," I said, "even if it did look like a nit on a gnat's ass. I think it was just shit-house luck. Dry clothes and decent chow is all I want now. Fuck all this bullshit."

We arrived back at the recruit depot in time for noon chow. It was almost beyond belief, as if the Marine Corps wanted to show appreciation to the heroes who had survived the carrot and chopsuey diet and performed their duty to God, Country, and the Corps. We were served steak, mashed potatoes, vegetables, fresh milk, and apple pie with ice cream. We gorged ourselves and kept chowing down.

After chow I would've traded my ass in hell to hit the sack for an hour, but that wasn't the way of the Corps. After a precious few minutes of flaking out on the deck in the barracks, it was, "Fall out, and fall in. Count off. Right-shoulder-arm. Right face. Forward, march." An afternoon of close order drill, organized grab ass, and running on a full stomach around the boondocks in loose sand was the order of the day.

After evening chow, which nobody seemed interested in, we were dragging ass big time. Everyone hit the sack and were stacking Z's before lights out, no bull sessions, poker, or letter writing.

About 0200 I woke up with a rumbling stomach cramp. Just a little gas, I figured; should pass in a minute. I started to...but thought, what if its not just gas? This might be the time when you can't trust a fart. It was raining and cold outside, and I didn't want to leave my warm sack and walk two hundred yards to the head, so I just tightened my pucker cord and went back to sleep. Another painful cramp rumbled around in my belly, so I decided to get dressed and take a walk. When my feet hit the deck I knew it wasn't just gas— no time to get dressed or even put on shoes. With dog tags flying I made a two-hundred-yard dash in record time. Evidently I wasn't the only one affected by two weeks of Chinese shit and carrots, followed by a glutinous, disgusting, overabundance of food. The head was full and overflowing with sick jarheads.

CHAPTER 26

RADAR SCHOOL

After boot training we were given aptitude tests to determine if we qualified for advanced training in any one of a number of skills. By reason of good luck and circumstances I qualified for Radar Technician school. I was able to correctly answer certain questions about electric circuitry, indicating I was a likely candidate. The reason I was able to answer certain questions about electric circuitry correctly was because my dad owned a small shop repairing electric motors. Over time, I had picked up enough knowledge to talk the talk but not necessarily enough to walk the walk. Evidently talking the talk was all that was necessary to qualify for school.

I was sent to Radar School at Wright Junior College in Chicago and was able to muddle through to nearly the end of the class when I met a WAVE. Her name was Joanne, and an affable relationship soon developed into something much more. Of course it was my fault it was happening so fast, but as it turned out she was seeing the instructor of the radar school I was attending. Chief Petty Officer Ramonski saw us together and thought it would be a good idea to kick my ass. Easier said than done. He ended up on the deck with a badly swollen cheek and a fat lip accompanied by a beautiful shiner, but he had the last word. The next day I received orders to report to the 7th Garrison at Camp Lejeune. He had pulled enough strings to get me kicked out of radar school and assigned to a Scout/Sniper outfit. I wondered what the duties of a Scout/Sniper were.

On the train to South Carolina I sat next to a marine and we introduced ourselves. "I'm on my way to Camp Lejeune to join up with the 7th Garrison," I said. "I'm gonna' be in a Scout/Sniper unit."

"No kidding, Olson. I got the same deal as you. I'm going to the 7th Garrison and I'm gonna be in a Scout/Sniper outfit too. Ain't that something? We're gonna be in the same outfit. How did you get that assignment?"

I told him about Joanne the WAVE and the fight with Romonski and getting kicked out of radar school.

"I was at that radar school, too, but I didn't stay very long."

"How come?"

"I went AWOL because I wanted to visit my dad and try to cheer him up. They wouldn't give me an emergency leave, so I went AWOL."

"How come you wanted to cheer up your dad?"

"My mom died about a year ago and my dad has been feeling pretty shitty ever since, and my sister, Ellie Mae, wrote me a letter and said he was feeling worse and if I could I should try to visit him."

"How come you couldn't get a leave to go visit him?"

"Because I just had a leave after boot camp, and I don't think they bought the story about my dad anyway."

"How was your dad when you saw him after boot camp?"

"Well, that's the thing, Olson. I didn't see him then. What happened was I got drunk in Oakland when the train stopped and I met this girl and we shacked up and I never did get home. I really felt bad about that and when my sister Ellie Mae told me my dad was in bad shape, I just said, "fuck it, I'm gonna go see him."

"How did the visit work out? Did you cheer him up?"

"Yeah, it was OK, but when I got back to Chicago the SP's arrested me and threw me in the brig at the Naval Station. I went before the man and got kicked out of radar school and assigned to the Scout/Sniper outfit."

"How come I never saw you at the radar school?"

"That's because I was just there a few days waiting for a class assignment when I decided to go AWOL to visit my dad to cheer him up, and I never did get into a class."

We arrived at Camp Lejeune, found the 7th Garrison headquarters, and were directed to the barracks housing the Scout/Sniper platoon. The platoon sergeant welcomed us aboard and assigned us bunks, telling us not to unpack our gear because we were leaving the following day for Quonset Point, Rhode Island, to board ship.

"Board ship to where, Sarg?" I asked.

"Beats me, Mac, they don't tell me shit."

CHAPTER 27

SHIPPING OUT

As we lined up on the dock to board ship my heart sank. I couldn't believe we were going to travel on that thing. *Where in hell did the Navy get that piece of crap?* I wondered. It was hard to imagine a ship that looked that bad could still be in service. It occurred to me that it might look that bad on the outside on purpose to fool the enemy so they wouldn't waste a torpedo on it, but that thought was dashed when I got onboard. It was worse inside than it looked from the outside. The hold we were to occupy had a combined smell of stale urine, vomit, and very bad body odor. The bunks we were going to occupy were stacked five high. I had the distinct feeling this wasn't going to be a pleasure cruise, and wondered what right they had sending us off to war on that disgusting excuse for a ship. They could at least have hosed it out, I remember thinking.

"What do ya' think, Dude?" I asked Reznik. "Do you think this tub will stay afloat long enough to get us to where ever in hell we're going?"

"If we're lucky; but you know what this reminds me of?" Reznik asked.

Not waiting for an answer, he continued, "What this whole deal reminds me of is being shanghaied, like in the old days, where they pick up drunks on the wharf like in Boston Harbor or London and throw a sack over their heads and haul their ass on board, tie em up and throw 'em below till they get to sea. Then they make 'em climb up the mast on a rope ladder to set the mainsail or whatever the hell it is they do up there."

"Where did you get such a dumb-assed idea as that?" I asked.

"It's not a dumb-assed idea. I saw it happen in a movie a couple years ago, and the more I think about it the more this deal reminds me of being shanghaied. Think about it, Olson. I was thrown in the brig at the Naval Station, shanghaied onto this bucket of bolts and sent to war with an outfit called Scout/Sniper. Now what in hell does that sound like to you?"

"Good point. I guess it's not such a dumb idea, now that I think about it. What do you think about this Scout/Sniper outfit? I talked to one of the guys when we were lined up on the dock waiting to board ship. What he told me sounded like bullshit. I don't think he knows any more than me. What have you heard?"

"I talked to the platoon sergeant," he answered, "and I don't like the way it sounds. What they do is, they put these Scout/Sniper guys on a Jap held island that's gonna be invaded by our guys, and what they're supposed to do is sneak in close and try to shoot an officer or anyone that looks important, and then haul ass."

"Well where do they haul ass to? And how do they get on the island if the Japs are already there? And how do they get off the island after they shoot an officer or someone who looks important? And wha—"

"Hold on, Olson. I don't know no more than you do. I just told you everything I know and it don't make no sense to me either. And another thing; I met some of the guys in this outfit, and they seemed pretty weird to me. I think we're in with a bunch of losers."

There was nothing I liked about the way things were shaping up. Scout/Sniper sounded like a one-way trip to oblivion, and that ship was probably the perfect way to get us there. I figured it was too late to apologize to Romonski for kicking his ass up between his eyeballs and get reinstated in radar school, and it was damn sure too late to drop out of the Marine Corps. My dad used to say, "Do the best you can with what you got. That's all any mule can do," or words to that effect.

After a few days at sea, sailing south off the East Coast, we got our first view of what war looked like. A freighter exploded and burst into flames, the likely victim of a torpedo from a German U-Boat. We continued on our way as if nothing at all had happened, but it sure got me thinking about the war. The fact that the Germans were able to send submarines all the way across the ocean to within a stone's throw of our shore and sink our ships just scared the crap right out of me.

The farther south we sailed the hotter it got, and it became absolutely unbearable below decks. After nine days of saltwater showers or no showers, the troops were definitely overripe.

On the tenth day we arrived at Liman Bay, the Atlantic entrance to the Panama Canal. We were informed we would have to wait our turn to start through, which could be several hours, but after going through three locks we would enter Catun Lake and be able to take fresh-water showers.

Six hours later, the ship moved into position and slowly proceeded through the locks. It was a fascinating two-hour experience. Fresh water began flowing through the pipes as we entered the lake, and the seldom-used shower stalls were now jammed with gyrenes trying to remove ten days of accumulated crud. Two locks after the Gillard Cut, our ship passed Balboa and joined a convoy in the Pacific.

Several days into our journey it was announced we were to cross the equator the following day. Crossing the equator was a big deal and a tradition of long standing in the Navy. The ceremonies consisted of those having previously crossed, known as Shellbacks, initiating those who had not crossed, known as Polliwogs. Ceremonies would commence at 0700 hours, and all Polliwogs were expected to participate. Those of us in the chow line chose to ignore the announcement, but as we exited the mess hall were grabbed and escorted to the number two hatch where a pool had been erected. We were forced to take off all our cloths and were blindfolded. A sticky crude oil was smeared on our heads and pubic hair. A rotten egg was shoved in my mouth, followed by a blow to my jaw. While gagging and trying to spit out the egg I was forced to walk the plank, which landed me in the pool full of stinking, rotten garbage. All in all it was a humiliating experience followed by an appearance in front of an ass-hole they called King Neptune.

"You are now a Shellback. Welcome to the Solemn Mysteries of the Ancient Order of the Deep!"

What a bunch of crap. Now I'm left with the impossible task of cleaning this crud out of my hair and from my crotch with saltwater soap. That sadistic sonofabitch who popped me in the jaw hit me way too hard.

The hot sultry, weather; the unlivable conditions below decks and the crotch problem, which itched non-stop, combined to make that voyage a nightmare experience. However, one should never assume things can't get worse. Two days after the Shellback bullshit it was announced that the ship had run out of food. For the last ten days of the trip we were rationed one hard-boiled egg and a cup of coffee for breakfast, no noon chow, and for evening chow one boiled potato and a cup of coffee. The hardboiled egg for breakfast was cold-storage, and if the yoke was green you could eat it but if it was blue it was rotten. I saw one poor hungry bastard unlucky enough to get a blue yoke. Instead of discarding it he wolfed it down. Big mistake. It wasn't long before he was heaving his guts out. There were many others who suffered the same fate.

CHAPTER 28

SAMOA

Ten days later, our poor excuse for a ship with a sadistic crew and no chow and not enough drinking water pulled into Pago Pago harbor at the island of Tutulia, Samoa. We had been at sea over thirty days since leaving the Panama Canal and were overjoyed to have arrived someplace-anyplace. As the ship slowly made its way to the dock, a gaggle of brown-skinned kids paddled out to meet us. They were shouting, "Tofa Malineee" in unison from their crudely fashioned boats. We assumed their mantra to be the Samoan version of "Aloha" but later learned, it could mean anything from "Hi," to "Give me a coin" or "Money" or in some cases "Please" or "Thank you" and possibly "Hello" or "Goodbye." One of the ship's crew, a salty old sailor who had been to Samoa before, tossed a coin over the side. Several of the little guys dove down for it, and one slender fellow popped up with it. Several of the Marines with coins tossed them to the kids until the ship was tied to the dock and the gangplank dropped.

I went below deck to get my gear but didn't have the strength to carry it all out in one trip, though I recall bringing it aboard in one trip without much of a problem. Others were trudging up and down the gangplank, also unable to carry all their gear at once. When ashore we were trucked to the camp vacated by the old Seventh Garrison. The quarters consisted of small, screened shacks with tin roofs.

Besides being near starvation I was in great need of water. We had been rationed two canteens per day on the voyage because the desalination plant on the ship wasn't working. As luck would have it, the water trailer had been parked about a half mile up the road from camp.

"Now why the hell do you suppose they parked the water trailer way the hell and gone up that dusty goddamn road?" Bellowed Reznik. "It ain't bad enough they starve us damn near to death on that fucking garbage scow and only give us two canteens of water a day but now they make us walk five miles just to get a drink. As far as I'm concerned this is pure, unadulterated bullshit."

"Gimme your canteen, Olson. I'm gonna go fill mine, and I might as well take yours too."

"I need the exercise," I said. "Maybe we can both walk up, and take a few canteens with us. Some of these guys look pretty beat up."

When we got back it was time for evening chow, which consisted of cooked K-rations. Even that tasted good after the egg-and-potato starvation diet.

Reznik asked. "How come we didn't get K-rations on the ship, Olson?"

"Beats the hell outa' me. Something's going on here that don't make sense."

The new Seventh Garrison assumed the duties of supposedly protecting the island from a Japanese invasion but consisted mostly of building back our physical strength and training for what would be the invasion of some island farther north. There were sixty of us in the Scout/Sniper platoon, and our time was spent learning the skills of stealth killing and precision shooting which is what Scout/Sniper training was all about. We were learning how to sneak up behind a person and with a knife in your right hand, throw your left arm under the chin of your victim, jerk him backwards, stab him in the heart or cut his throat-your choice. Then there's the one with a short length of twine used to strangle someone from behind.

Everyone had to turn in his M1 Garand rifle and were issued a carbine as a replacement. The carbine was a lightweight weapon, which felt like a toy compared to the Garand, and didn't have the range of the Garand. I was having a hard time hitting an eight-inch bull at two hundred yards, which I could do all day with my Garand. The only advantage to the carbine was that it had a fifteen-round clip and didn't weigh as much. I was sorry I had to make the change, but maybe later I'd be glad when I got used to it. In any event, I had no say in the matter.

Reznik and I discussed the training we were receiving and concluded this Scout/ Sniper thing was pretty much a one-way ticket to never-never land. The question I had in my mind was the one I originally had. If they plan on putting us on an island occupied by Japanese forces to sneak up and kill an officer or someone important or destroy equipment, how are we supposed to get off the island? I put that question to the sergeant training us, but didn't get a definitive answer. I took his non-answer to mean that we probably wouldn't get off the island, at least not alive.

Contact with the locals was limited due to the lack of time because of the extensive combat training we were receiving. However, several of the guys were slipping into the village at night when we learned that SPAM was highly valuable and could be used as a medium of exchange. They called it "poo soop oo." A can of SPAM could buy a pint of "Tubaa," a jungle booze distilled from the meat and milk of coconuts. It could also purchase laundry service, native crafted pieces de'art or the temporary affection, of a local lass.

We learned a few words of their language. As mentioned earlier, Tofa had a variety of meanings. "Muca Muca" meant, "See," or "I see," or "Let me see." "Su su" referred to a woman's breast. It didn't take long for the guys to pick up on, "Muca Muca su su."The girls took this as a compliment and gladly complied.

The ideal way to spend an evening was to be invited to the home or "fahlie" of a local family. The marine brought a can of poo soop oo, and the father of the family supplied the tubaa. It was party time, which meant sitting around singing. "Samoha ah Samoha, saea me my mmooah." We assumed that was their national anthem. They really got into, "You Are My Sunshine," and never tired of singing that song.

Three weeks into 'killing school', I was told to report to Lieutenant Colonel Amend.

I was ushered into his office by the battalion clerk and stood at attention in front of his desk, feeling somewhat uncomfortable. I was pretty sure he didn't invite me in to ask if there was anything he could do to make my life more pleasurable. I figured the only reason for me to be there was because I had done something wrong, but for the life of me I couldn't imagine what it was. So far I had done everything I was supposed to do. I experienced all the pain and suffering of the voyage, including almost starving to death. I went through all their training exercises there, learning all the different ways to kill a person, and was willing to do so. What the hell could I have done that didn't measure up? I wondered.

"At ease, private," the Colonel said. "According to your service jacket, you attended Radar School at Wright Junior College in Chicago. What the hell are you doing in a Scout/Sniper outfit? That's for fuck-ups and misfits; are you a fuck-up or a misfit?"

At the mention of radar school I became alert. I wondered what this was all about, and if opportunity was knocking.

"Well are you, or aren't you?" he asked.

"Excuse me sir, are I or aren't I what?"

"Are you a fuck-up or aren't you a fuck-up? That's a simple enough question, isn't it?"

"Yes sir, that is a simple enough question, and the answer is no, I'm not a fuck-up. I consider being in the Corps an honor and don't intend to ever be a fuck-up, sir," I answered with as much ass-kissing deference to his rank as I could muster.

"Well then," he continued, "did you finish radar school?"

I need to be very careful here. The way I handle this conversation could be a matter of life or death for me because it could be a ticket out of the suicide squad. He obviously is interested in what I know or what he thinks I know about radar. If that's going to be a key to getting out of Scout/Sniper, I intend to tell whatever lies are necessary to make that happen. I remember my dad telling me one time, "Don't lie, but if you do, make it believable," or words to that effect.

"Sir, I did not graduate from radar school."

"Why was that?"

I figure telling him I got kicked out because of a fight with the instructor over a WAVE is not what he would want to hear, so I need to come up with something better than that, and I need to come up with it right now.

"Sir, the Chief Petty Officer instructor was a genuine first-class ass-hole. He was a good enough instructor and he knew what he was talking about, and I learned all about radar maintenance and operation. The problem was, he didn't like me, probably because I was a marine, and I Goddamned sure didn't like him. I always had an answer for him and I got good grades on the progress tests, which seemed to piss him off. He continually tried to catch me in a wrong answer, but he never could."

"Well, they don't just kick you out of school because you do good, so what happened?"

"What happened, sir, was he changed some of my answers on the final exam, and I flunked the test. When I found out what he had done I got pissed off and decked the sonofabitch. The next day I received orders to report to Camp Lejeune for assignment to a Scout/Sniper unit."

He stared at me for what seemed a long time but was probably just a few seconds, then said, "Olson, I need radar technicians in the worst way, and I want to believe I was just blessed with one, so I choose to believe you. However, if I find you've fed me a line of crap I guarantee you'll live to regret it. Do you understand what I'm telling you?"

"Sir, I do understand what your saying. What I just told you is true. I don't know what else I can say, sir."

"Very well. However, I have one more question. Did you finish the course? You said earlier you didn't graduate but did you finish the course? There's nothing in your service jacket to indicate that; just that you attended the school."

Well, now, ain't that a hoot? Nothing in my record! That means I can tell him anything and all that bullshit I just dumped on him was unnecessary, but now I gotta follow through. So far I've only needed to lie about what the fight with Chief Romonski was really all about and

I think he bought that. I should be able to almost tell the truth on this question-not quite but almost. Actually, I almost finished the course, but I don't think he wants to hear "almost."

"I did finish the course, sir, but after I popped the instructor he had me transferred out the next day."

"Very well, Olson. You'll become part of our radar program."

Was I hearing right? I was familiar with the ways of the Corps and figured if they knew you wanted a particular assignment you could be pretty damn sure you'd get just the opposite. For instance, if you wanted to be an airplane mechanic they'd probably make you a machine-gunner. If you wanted an East Coast assignment you could be pretty sure you'd be sent to the West Coast. I was afraid if this guy knew I wanted out of the Scout/Sniper platoon in the worst way he might keep me there even though he needed radar technicians. That was basic Marine Corps logic.

"Sir, if it's all the same to you, I prefer the excitement of being a Scout/Sniper to the boredom of staring at a radar screen."

"Private, what assignments you receive, where you're sent, and what happens to you is decided for you, not by you. You have absolutely no choice in these matters. I hope you understand that."

That worked better than I thought it would.

"Yes, sir, I do understand that."

"Private Olson, we need technicians. I'm assigning you to a 270-dog outfit."

I figured that would be a good time for me to prove to myself how smart I was, by showing my ignorance.

"Sir, what is a 270-dog? I don't know a damn thing about dogs."

He bristled and sharply asked, "Private, are you trying to be funny?"

"Not at all, sir," I answered with as much sincerity as I could muster.

"A 270-D is a long-range radar. Dog signifies D, just as Charley signifies C. This is done to eliminate mistaking D from C, E, G, P, T, V, or Z, because they all sound alike. Do you understand that?"

"Yes, sir, I do understand that, since you just explained it so well. Thank you, sir."

"Carry on private."

"Aye aye, sir," I said as I did a smart about-face and exited his office.

To the clerk he said, "Corporal, escort Private Olson to Lieutenant Pickering's office. He is to be attached to the 2nd AAA Battalion, and when you return advise Private Reznik he's to report to me at 0900 hours, tomorrow."

Back in our hut that night, Reznik said, "You say he's gonna call me in? Dude, I don't know shit about radar, remember? I didn't even go to a class before I went AWOL. If he asked me what a radar was I'd have to admit I don't even know what one looks like."

"Reznik, I know that, and you know that, but Mister Big doesn't know that. We gotta keep it that way. All he knows is your last assignment was at radar school. He doesn't know if you were in the class one day or three months. What you need to understand is, your service jacket doesn't have any details. It just says where you were assigned, not what you did or how long you were there."

"How do you know that, Olson?"

"I know that because of the interview I just had with the Colonel. He said my service jacket didn't have any details, and asked if I finished the class. I told him I finished the class but decked the instructor and got transferred to Camp Lejeune. Actually, he believed what he wanted to believe because he wants radar operators so bad he can taste it," I explained.

"Olson, if you could explain some of the details about how radar works I might feel more comfortable trying to bullshit my way through this."

"OK, but first let me ask you something. I qualified for Radar School because my dad fixed electric motors and I picked up a few of the terms from him so was able to answer some of the questions, which, for some reason, qualified me for Radar School. I have to admit it was a fluke. My question to you is, what did you do to qualify?"

"I didn't do shit, Olson. I been trying to figure it out too. What I think happened is, I think they got my name mixed up with someone named 'Rasnik' and sent me to that school instead of him."

"Why do you think they got your name mixed up with someone named Rasnik?

"Because that's the name they had on my orders to send me to this Scout/Sniper outfit. When I pointed out their mistake, they changed the name on my orders."

"Makes sense to me. Sounds like you figured it out."

"So, Olson, how about putting me in touch with what radar is all about so I can convince the Colonel I know something I don't know."

"Sure. I was in school long enough to learn the basics but not much more. The technical stuff went right over my head, but operating a radar isn't all that complicated. Radar is a system of sending out an electronic beam. When the beam hits something like an airplane or a ship, the signal bounces back to the receiver. The direction of the object and the time it takes the signal to return are measured to determine how far out the object is and what its course is. The radar operator controls the radar operation by looking through a scope and working the various dials, buttons, and other controls. When he sees a blip on the screen, he determines the coordinates and reads them off to a person plotting the movement of the aircraft or ship, or whatever they're tracking." I explained.

"Well, OK, Olson, that helps a lot, and I feel better already. What else does the radar dude need to know?"

"First off, don't refer to him as the radar dude. He's a Radar Technician, and his responsibility is to keep the radar gear functioning."

"OK, I gotcha.' What else should I know?"

"Nothing about radar; the main thing is how you deal with Colonel...What the fuck's his name? Oh yeah, Amend– Colonel Amend. You need to show a great deal of respect. Say 'sir' a lot. Sir, sir, sir. All them guys love that shit. It makes 'em feel important and tells them that you know they're better than you because they don't have to say 'sir' to you. However, don't go overboard either. Just try to be believable. Another thing, and this is important: Don't offer anything."

"What do you mean, don't offer him anything? Did you think I was going to offer the ass hole a cigarette or a stick of gum, or something like that?"

"Hell no, dummy, I didn't mean that. I mean don't offer any information he doesn't ask for. Say as little as possible."

"OK, Olson. I got it; but you need to be careful about that dummy stuff. I've decked bigger bozos than you for less."

"Calm down; I'm trying to be helpful; but any time you want to duke it out just say so, and we'll see who gets knocked on his ass."

That night we got the shit scared out of us. The 155 Long Tom batteries, which were strung out along the beach, opened up a tremendous barrage. The sound of all those guns firing off, even at intervals, was indescribable. We were just thirty yards behind the guns, and the concussion was so great it blew the tin roofs off our huts. We thought the Japs were coming, and it was a mad scramble to gather up our rifles and ammo and try to get organized into some semblance of a fighting unit. I guess the artillery guys just wanted to see if their guns worked.

At morning muster, Reznik was told to report to Colonel Amend, and it wasn't until noon chow that I was able to catch up with him.

"How did it go, Dude?"

"No problem. He only asked a few simple questions. He had the company clerk take me over to the 2nd AAA Battalion Headquarters and I reported in to Sergeant Smyth. That was it."

"What did he ask you?"

"He asked me if I went to the radar school in Chicago. Answer, yes.

"He asked if I finished the class. Answer, no.

"He asked why. Answer, I went AWOL to visit my dad, who was dying, and they wouldn't give me an emergency leave. When I got back to Chicago the SP's arrested me, and I got kicked out of radar school and assigned to this outfit.

"He asked me if I knew how to operate and repair radar. Answer, yes.

"End of interview."

"Well, ain't you just the slick sonofabitch," I said, patting him on the back. "Looks like we angled our way out of the death squad. All we gotta do now is kick back and watch a radar screen and enjoy the rest of the war."

"Yeah, you're probably right, Olson. I figure the worst of the war is over for us. I think we oughta celebrate. Let's slip on down to the village and get drunk on that tubaa crap. If we're lucky, we might get laid."

"Good idea, Dude, but it's not about luck. It's about SPAM."

CHAPTER 29

TARAWA

November 1, 1943 we queued up at the dock and boarded a freighter/ troop transport to sail into history. The natives sang, "Tofaa Malinee Alloofayah," which means "Come back for your kids." The ship reminded me of the tub that took us from Quonset Point to Samoa; not quite as bad but almost. It was sure not the Queen Mary, but nevertheless part of a huge convoy heading north. We were told later we were going to the Gilbert Islands to be part of the invasion of Tarawa, whatever or wherever that was.

A week out, we were wishing we were back at Samoa. The weather was unbearably hot, and nowhere could we find relief. On deck, the sun blazed down on us unmercifully, and shade was almost nonexistent; what little there was, was in great demand. Below decks was just as hot but many times worse as there was no movement of air and was a stifling, stinking rat hole. That's where we went when GQ (general quarters) sounded. There was no way we could remain on deck when the ship's crew was manning their battle stations. Below decks there was no room to wander about, so it was necessary that everyone stay in his bunk. The bunks were stacked five high and were nothing more than a piece of canvas secured into a metal frame. The cute thing about them was they were stacked so close together you only had enough room to lie on your back or on your stomach. In terms of the worst place in the world to be, this would get my vote. The only thing that could have made it worse would have been a set of leg irons.

A boxing ring was set up on a hatch cover, and a couple guys put on the gloves. They only lasted one round before the sun decked them both. A black ship's Cook wanted someone to get in the ring with him—anyone it seemed. He wasn't able to interest an opponent, and no amount of chiding was working. Reznik decided it would be just funny as hell to see this guy kick my ass. No way was I going to let that happen. I had carved out a small piece of shade up against the rear wheel of a truck and I had no intention of giving it up. I was barely staying alive in that heat as it was, but goddamn it, Reznik and the black guy kept goading me, and then the others joined in the chorus until I agreed. It was the only way I could maintain any self-respect; besides, that guy was pissing me off.

I slipped my hands into the sweaty gloves, and Reznik happily laced them up for me. I climbed into the ring, but my heart wasn't in the fight. I wanted it to be over as soon as possible, even if I went down with the first punch and didn't get up. A mess cook banged a soup ladle against a pan, and the match was on. As we sparred around, sizing each other up, I got the distinct feeling this wasn't going to be the friendly sparing match I was promised. I saw a rare opening and decided to take advantage of it and maybe end the fight. I landed a powerful right hand to his mouth, and he went down spurting blood. Hooray for me. Now I could return to my reserved spot in the shade, which was part of the deal. I hoped he would stay down, but no such luck. He bounced up like a rubber ball and proceeded to give me a hands-on demonstration in the fine art of boxing, which was not soon forgotten. In quick succession he tagged me with four or five left jabs, and I didn't even see the blow that decked me. My buddies dragged me back to my reserved seat in the shade as I gasped for air. That was not fun. I got a sandwich but he got a three-course meal and I felt like shit.

Later that evening I met up with Mister Tough Guy on deck.

"I been lookn' for you." He said.

"Get lost champ; I ain't in no mood to fight."

"No. No boxing. I got something for you. You hungry?"

Not waiting for an answer, he said, "I swiped some chow from the officers mess. Come on down to my cabin."

I had nothing to lose and maybe something to gain, so of course I agreed. The guy's cabin was no luxury suite, barely wide enough to walk alongside his bunk. The bulkheads were plastered with pictures and news clippings of him known as "Killer Black." Damn, that guy was a pro. If I had known that I damn sure wouldn't have crawled into the ring with him. Before I had a chance to tell him what an ass-hole I thought he was he handed me a flank of ham.

"Well, holy shit, Dude, are you giving this to me?"

I couldn't believe my good fortune. I stuck my hand out and said, "Put it there, pal; you're a life saver. You don't know how hungry we are."

"Yes, I do. I'm a ship's cook and we all know you guys are on short rations. We delivered a boat-load of Marines to the Canal during that campaign, and I heard that most of them got killed. This convoy is headed for Tarawa, and if it's going to be as bad as it was at Guadalcanal, you guys got some real bad shit ahead of you."

I shared the ham with some of the guys in my platoon. We all figured we had gone to heaven without dying. "Killer Black" made several more contributions while on our journey to Tarawa, making the trip more pleasurable for us than it otherwise would have been.

We had to be kept in good shape so were put through a daily exercise regimen. We also attended lectures designed to orient us to what might lie ahead. We studied a map of the atoll we were to land on, known as Betio, in the Tarawa group of the Gilbert Islands. The planned order of action, we were told, was for the big guns of the Navy battlewagons and cruisers to bombard the island, alternating with Navy dive bombers, both designed to soften up the enemy strongholds. Next step was the landing of the Marines, off-loaded from troop transports to Higgins boats by way of cargo nets hung down the side of the ship. The Higgins boats were to deliver the Marines to the beach, where we would engage the enemy.

The convoy seemed to grow by several ships overnight, and rumor had it we were close to our destination. The troops were getting nervous and apprehensive about what was in store for them. There was a lot of meaningless chatter to cover the fear we felt. We were trying to anticipate what facing the enemy was going to be like.

There was a lot of bravado talk about killing the Japs, probably from those most frightened.

GQ sounded, and there was a mad scramble among the ship's crew to get to their battle stations, and for the troops to get below decks for lock down. Out of the sky several Japanese planes were spotted diving toward the convoy. We were moving as quickly as we could to get below, but a crowd that size could move only so fast. Through all this tumult was the sound of an airplane screaming toward us with guns blazing, and the guns from our ship returning fire. It was over so fast no one had a chance to be frightened, but we did get an idea what it was like to be shot at.

We heard later that a member of a gun crew had been killed. He was known as "Killer Black," a fairly well known boxer.

Twenty days after leaving Samoa, at 0300 hours, we were ordered to fall in topside and were pleasantly surprised to be served steak for breakfast, the best meal yet on that ship. After morning chow we strapped on our knapsack, haversack, web belt with ammo clips, bayonet, kabar knife, blanket, trenching tool, and two extra bandoleers of ammunition. With helmet, K rations, and a couple canteens of water, each man was packing about sixty pounds.

While waiting our turn to go down the net we watched the fireworks show as the Navy was shelling the island with their big guns.

CHAPTER 30

FROM DREAMLAND TO REALITY

"What's that guy saying? Where am I?"

"Wake up, Mac, you're relieved. Here, let me help you out of this hole."

Now I remember; I'm still in this stinking foxhole. I can't believe it. I'm getting off the line. I hope I don't die before I get to a hospital. I've never been this sick. I'm shaking all over and I'm so damn weak I can't move.

"Corpsman. Over here; bring a stretcher. This guy can't get up, and he's too big for me to carry."

So ended my stay on the Shuri Castle/Naha City battle line.

I was taken to the field hospital and pointed toward the shower. After the most enjoyable shower I ever had I was placed in a ward along with others suffering from dengue fever, malaria, malnutrition, exhaustion, and confusion. I have little recollection of the first several days and for some time afterward had trouble separating reality from dreams. I remember alternating between burning up with fever at times and shaking with cold at other times. I experienced outlandish and frightening dreams, which seemed to go on forever. Even with all that, I was one of the lucky ones. Each day one or two were turned over to Grave Registration.

For me the treatment was the right medicine because one morning I woke out of a peaceful sleep, all signs of fever gone, but still feeling weak. The nightmarish dreams, which had accompanied the fever, had also disappeared. I was grateful to still be alive and thanked God for my recovery. It took a while to separate the incident of shooting Reznik in the arm from the weird dreams I had been having. When I finally came to grips with that reality I felt terrible, remembering that the whole, stupid idea had been mine.

When I was discharged from the hospital I rejoined what was left of my company. We had lost so many men we were no longer a tactical unit. Of the sixty-five in my platoon only five of us survived. The others were either killed or wounded or too sick for duty. The strength of our company was reduced to twenty-five of the original two hundred eighty. We were sent north to the Yontan Airfield to await further orders and replacements to fill the empty ranks of our company.

At Yontan we reported to Captain Clyde.

"Is this all that's left of your platoon, Sergeant?" he asked Cleat.

"Yes, sir, it is," Cleat answered, then added, "We took it in the skivvies big time at Naha. What the hell happened, sir? They just left us out there to die. How come we didn't get relieved?"

"A lot of things happened, Sergeant," the captain answered. "The Japs were tougher than we thought, and as you know they fight until the last soldier is dead. The replacements were over a week late; we still don't know why. I'm glad you all made it this far and I hope you live through the rest of the war and that you get home alive."

He looked at me and said, "How you doing, Olson? I see you came out on the other side of the prune wine incident at Guam."

"Yes, sir, I did. Where do we go from here, Captain?"

"There's an Okinawan tomb about a half mile west of here. Bivouac there until we call you. Your platoon will be built up to full strength and you'll be assigned the task of protecting the radar here at Yontan. I hope it'll be an easy assignment. You deserve it."

"One more thing, sir. I'd like to ask a favor of you."

"What is it, Corporal?"

"My buddy took a round on the Naha line, and I don't know if he's still alive. If he's not dead, could you find out where he was sent?"

"Certainly, Olson, give me his full name, and when I learn something I'll have your platoon leader pass it along to you."

"Thank you, sir. I really appreciate it. His name is Louis Reznik."

We found the burial vault, inspected it, and concluded it would be a great place to spend the rest of the war, but knew that wouldn't be the case. The concrete tomb was cut into the side of a hill. The interior was about fifteen feet square, with wide steps leading up to the two-foot-high by two-foot-wide entrance. On the steps were jugs containing the bones of long-gone Okinawans. Over the entrance was a foot-thick concrete domed roof, and in front of the tomb was a yard surrounded by a three-foot-high, stonewall. We moved the jugs to a safe location a short distance away and gave the room a squirt from a flame thrower to kill the bugs before moving in. The new digs provided excellent protection against artillery and bomb shrapnel.

This was a time for much needed R&R for us. The Japanese had committed all their forces to the battles in the south, leaving the occupation of the airfield mostly uncontested. The only problem we had to contend with was "Piss Call Charlie." Every evening between sundown and dark the Japanese sent a Zero over the airfield and surrounding area to strafe and bomb. It was a quick in-and-out raid. On our second day at the tomb we were spotted by the pilot who decided we'd be his target of choice for that evening.

Schuber and Cleat had just returned from the water trailer, each with a helmet full of water, and were in the process of soaping up for a "douche" when Charley started his run. Hillman saw him first and yelled, "Hit the deck. Here comes Charley!"

Hillman and I jumped behind the stone wall while Schuber and Cleat dove for the opening of the tomb, since it was closest for them. They hit the opening at the same time, and it being just two-feet square, could not accommodate them both. There they were, hopelessly stuck with their upper bodies inside the tomb and their lower halves outside. What a picture that was.

Charley came in with all guns blazing, but then a strange thing happened. He stopped shooting just short of the wall, peeled off and flew away. When Charley was gone and we were damn sure he was gone, Riley and Hillman and I spent the next thirty minutes prying the other two loose, skinning them up pretty bad in the process.

We didn't understand why Charlie aborted his run but decided he either ran out of ammunition or the tomb was a religious shrine and he didn't want to desecrate it. Hillman suggested the reason he pulled out was because he had a sense of humor.

After three weeks the radar installation was complete so we joined our company, which had been brought up to strength from the remnants of other companies who had participated in the Naha battle as well as replacements newly arrived from the States. Our platoon was assigned the task of protecting the radar, which I figured should be an easy touch. How hard could it be guarding a radar station? I remember thinking.

CHAPTER 31

THE BLACK ROBE AFFAIR

Our job of guarding the radar was but a small part of a larger picture. The Japanese had assigned considerable resources to recapturing or destroying the airfield as the Army Air Corps was conducting bombing sorties against the mainland of Japan. The Japanese were launching bombing strikes on the airfield and sending ground patrols against the Marine defenders at night. Our duties consisted of dusk-to-dawn security watches by night and search-and-kill patrols by day to defend against these activities. It had all the elements of a full-blown war, invalidating any dreams we might have had for an easy assignment. After three weeks of this combat we lost forty-eight of the original sixty-five men killed or wounded. The hunt-and-kill patrols were discontinued so we could concentrate our forces against the nightly attacks.

Our days were divided between sleeping, eating, and "strumming the banjo." Sandbag walls had to be repaired after every night's activities. While waiting for replacements we did double duty because of the shortage of personnel. My battle station was in a foxhole about fifteen yards from a .50 caliber machine gun emplacement. My extra job was to assist DeGroot, the gunner, when we were being bombed. His partner had been killed a couple days before. When the bombs start falling I was to leave my foxhole and haul ass over to the .50 caliber and help the gunner by placing drums of ammunition in the gun clips while he was firing at the aircraft.

One night at about 0200 when the moon was out the enemy started their bombing run. I vacated my hole to join the gunner. Bombs were falling all around, and as I dove into the sandbag enclosure the gunner caught a large piece of shrapnel to his face and was instantly killed. My job description changed from machinegun loader to machinegun loader and machinegun gunner. I moved DeGroot out of the way and took over my new job, firing a couple short bursts as the aircraft passed over and out of range.

DeGroot was a mess. Not only did he not have a face anymore, but most of his head was splattered all over his gun. I moved him out of the enclosure, laid him down and covered him with my field jacket, then cleaned as much of his head off the gun as I could.

All was quiet for a while and I thought the rest of the night would go by without further action. Wrong.

I was about to experience a very strange and troubling event. It started as a murmuring sound, like a group of people, all trying to talk at the same time. I thought my ears were playing tricks on me, or possibly my mind had snapped. I wasn't reassured when I looked over the sandbag wall and by the light of the moon saw what appeared to be the vague outline of a very large group of people. They were about five hundred yards away, down a depressed valley, walking very slowly toward our lines. That activity didn't resemble any military procedure I had ever seen. Panic set in. I didn't know what to make of this strange event. I yelled, "Halt!" They kept coming. Again, "Halt! Who Goes There?" No response. The others in foxholes were franticly yelling for them to halt, but to no avail. They just continued their slow advance toward our lines, the chanting getting louder as they got closer. It was downright spooky, and I was very near to panicking. What to do? Level this big gun just over their heads and give them a short burst. *That should do it,* I thought. I tried to adjust the gun down, but the sandbags wouldn't allow that to happen. The gun was only meant to fire up at enemy aircraft. They were getting closer as I frantically pulled sandbags out of the way. Other guys from foxholes and gun emplacements were yelling. "Halt. Halt or we'll shoot." They kept coming. I finally removed enough sandbags to adjust the gun toward them. As they got closer, I was able to see them more clearly. They were all dressed in black clothing, with black hoods covering their heads. They slowly walked toward us, continuing their chanting. That was just too spooky. I let loose a burst over their heads, which I figured should stop them, but instead triggered an outburst of gunfire from several different gun emplacements and foxholes. The other guys were scared and as spooked about that whole episode as I was. Evidently they were zeroing in on the "black hoods," not just firing over their heads. The screaming could barely be heard above the chattering noise of the guns. The whole thing lasted about one minute, than all was quiet.

I placed another drum of ammunition on the gun in anticipation of more enemy action, if that's what that was. The rest of the night was quiet and I had a couple hours to think about what had happened. I relived the scene of all those people walking toward us, mumbling or chanting. It all sounded the same- just meaningless sounds.

And the way they were dressed, what the hell was that all about? Looked like black gowns with hoods covering their heads. I wonder if they are all dead. What if some of them are still alive and are going to jump in over the sandbags and hack me up? What if they weren't real? What if they were ghosts and weird stuff was going to happen to us? Damn, there I go again, dreaming up all kinds of crap and spooking myself out. I don't believe any of that hokey-pokey stuff, so why am I thinking it? They might be Japanese soldiers dressed up like that, trying to freak us out. Well, they damn sure freaked me out; all the other guys too. I wonder if they thought we'd just roll over and die of fright and if we didn't die of fright, would we just sit there too stunned to shoot?

That whole thing was driving me nuts because it made no sense.

Dawn at last and my watch ended. I hustled down the hill to look at the carnage and try to figure out what had happened. I wasn't prepared for what I found. I had seen many dead, wounded, and mangled people in the war, but what I saw was beyond anything I had ever seen or could ever imagine. The bodies weren't only dead, they were chewed up beyond anything recognizable. I couldn't help wondering if there were any women or children among them. It was a terrible scene, and though I hadn't eaten since the night before, bent over and vomited on an empty stomach. The others arrived, staring at the scene in silence and disbelief. Two or three of the new guys reacted as I had. Some others were crying unashamedly. Still others were on their knees, praying. It was just too horrible to describe.

The war up until that time had been on an impersonal level in terms of the enemy. They were soldiers and we were soldiers, each trying to kill the other. When I stood there looking at that mass of slaughtered humanity I was forced to look at the war from another perspective. These people, I felt, were not the enemy. They surely had nothing to do with the war and probably thought of us as invaders of their homeland. Their walk toward our guns might very well have been a gesture of peace, though certainly ill-advised. They might not have had any idea that the leaders of their country were the perpetrators of the war and all the death and destruction was on their heads.

Shortly, several officers arrived. We were questioned about what had happened, and explained as best we could, but of course our answers didn't shed light on the strange and bizarre happenings of that night. Although the bodies were badly chewed up, it was determined by the officers that under the robes were Japanese uniforms. The question remained; what did they hope to accomplish by that weird activity? Were the participants Japanese soldiers, or civilians, perhaps women or even children? Maybe they were monks, and the mumblings were chants. What were they saying? Whatever their message, none of us understood it.

To no one in particular, but perhaps to all present, I said, "This is war, and your people started it. What the hell were we supposed to do, just sit here and see what would happen? How did we know you didn't have guns? Nothing like this has ever happened before. What were you trying to do? You should have stayed in your church. It's a tough, godawful, goddamn war. You can chant and pray all you want, but you're not going to change that!"

When the Chaplain arrived on the scene, he dropped to his knees in prayer, where he remained for several minutes.

The Colonel was heard to say to another officer, "Get a bulldozer in here and cover up these poor bastards."

Nothing more was ever said or done about that incident, but was *never* to be forgotten by any of us in the foxholes that night.

One would think after that experience you wouldn't be able to eat or sleep, and might be a little whacked out by the whole thing. Not so. After a shower I was hungry enough to eat the tail end out of a skunk. I met Pop Schuber for morning chow.

"What did you think of that shit last night, Pop? Wasn't that something?" It was the damndest thing I ever seen, and I hope I never see anything like it again. Did you see the way our fire chewed up those people?

"Dude, I didn't see nothin'. After the fireworks I headed back to the tent when our watch was up. I can imagine what it looked like, but I damn sure didn't want to see it. I got enough ghosts up here; I don't need no more."

CHAPTER 32

PRESIDENT ROOSEVELT

We heard President Roosevelt had died of natural causes. A few of the guys were all grieved out about it, but I couldn't get all that worked up. It seemed to me they should have been grieving over their buddies who were dead and dying every day in a war they didn't have anything to do with starting, instead of for the guy who could have done something about preventing it in the first place. I remember in the thirties reading about us selling scrap metal to Japan. It was assumed by everyone that they would use it to build warships and tanks. Now who did the President think they intended to use those warships and tanks against if not The United States? Another thing I thought a lot about was, how come we had to go over to Europe and fight that war for those countries? That's another thing I remember reading a lot about in the thirties. Hitler was building up his war machine, and none of his neighbors were doing a damn thing about it. I wondered who they thought was going to be on the wrong end of his guns. It seemed to me that if they all had gotten together and countered Hitler's arms buildup with one of their own, they probably wouldn't have had the war. But if they did have the war, they should, and probably could have fought it themselves. We wouldn't have had to go over there and fight it for them.

Mail call brought me a letter from Reznik.

Hi Olson,

I got flown out of Okinawa after you shot me in the arm.
I'm in a hospital in Hawaii living the good life. I'm damn
glad to be here that's for sure and if you was here I would
kick your ass up there between your eyeballs for what you
done to me. I guess it was my fault to but I would kick
your ass anyway but you would have had to tie one arm
behind your back to make it even. That's right buddy they
had to whack my arm off. I am glad it was not my left
arm. Write me a letter and tell me what is going on. If I
get this letter back marked deceased I will know you got
killed in that fucking hole.

Your foxhole buddy,
Louis Reznick

CHAPTER 33

FIVE MORE MINUTES

After the black robe affair I figured I had about run the gamut on all the horrors the goddamn war could possibly throw at me, but I suppose the operative word is 'about.' There was still more to come. The enemy seemed intent on retaking Yonton Airfield as they were receiving air-raids on their homeland from here. To accomplish that, they were bringing in reinforcements from the south to throw against our meager defences.

One particularly distressful security watch stands out in my mind.

I had spent part of the day digging three foxholes to prepare for the night ahead, and had settled into hole number one for the long, dark, and lonely night. In the hours before midnight I was alert to all the sounds of the night around me, but from midnight till dawn my mind was playing tricks on me as I desperately fought off sleep. Each movement and sound, real or imagined, I thought to be that of a Japanese soldier about to join me, knife in hand. I was terrified by the thoughts that raced through my mind, not expecting to live much longer, almost wishing it would end. I was plagued with the memories of a particularly disturbing night in a two-man foxhole on Tarawa. I was never able to pull a dusk-to-dawn watch without going over in my mind every detail of that night. The memories were both good and bad; good in that I had learned first-hand and early on what the enemy was capable of, and being armed with that knowledge, would never be caught unprepared, either physically or mentally; bad in that I was burdened with those thoughts probably to my detriment. I imagined a Japanese soldier naked save for a loincloth rolling into my foxhole with a knife in each hand stabbing and hacking me to death.

How many girls have I scored with? Now why the hell did I think of that? Probably because it's been so long since I enjoyed those pleasures and they dominate so much of my thoughts. Better not think of those things, it just makes matters worse. I wonder how my brother felt when he got shot in Italy. What is the quickest, least painful way to die? I want to get drunk and stay unconscious until this brutal war is over. I'll probably be dead in five minutes. Hell, even if I live I'll still be on Okinawa without women or anything else that makes life worth living. Worse yet, I'll probably be part of the invasion of Japan; I know I won't live through that battle.

Damn, I'm dry. It feels like my mouth's full of cotton. If I reach for my canteen the noise or movement might tip off my position. It's impossible to drink from a canteen silently. The guy who designed them must have had his head up his ass. Why couldn't he have put a rubber lid on them, and something other than a metal chain? You need to hold the canteen with one hand and the lid and chain with the other while drinking, and if you allow the lid to slip out of your hand and it hits the canteen it's like ringing a cowbell. That certainly isn't the signal I want to send to the enemy.

They could be a couple yards from me right now. I'll keep sucking on this pebble. Maybe I still have five minutes. Damn, I'm scared. There's no moon tonight and it's pitch black; it's even hard to breathe this black air. Can they hear me breathing? If I stop breathing maybe I can hear them. It's a lonesome, spooky war. Wish I had someone to cover my back. Maybe this blackness is a good thing. If I can't see them, they can't see me. I wonder if they can smell me. We didn't bury the dead Japs very deep; maybe they'll mask my smell. I think I'm going crazy. Maybe I'll jump out of this fucking hole and run toward them, yelling "Bonsai!" They'll shoot me, and it'll be all over. Damn, it's dark. I'm too scared to move, and I'm thirsty. These goddamn fleas and mosquitoes are driving me nuts. Wish my eyes would adjust. How am I going to get it? Hope it's a clean head shot; I want it quick and neat. Sid got his throat slashed last night. I sure as hell don't want to go out that way. He was a mess— a gruesome bloody goddamn mess; couple guys puked when they saw him.

There was a muzzle flash, and a slug hit a sandbag near my face. Sand stung as it bit into my cheek. They spotted me. My heart began pounding as panic set in.

I fired a burst in the direction of the muzzle flash and dove for another foxhole a few feet away. Grenades exploded in the hole I just vacated. I lobbed two grenades toward their position as fast as I could pull the pins.

It became very quiet and seemed darker because the flash of the explosions had blinded me, and I couldn't hear anything except the ringing in my ears. The acrid fumes of burned gunpowder and dust choked me and I couldn't get my breath. It felt like a huge rubber band was around my chest. I was wet and clammy from fear.

Come on, eyes, ears, let me know what's out there. Someone's near. I know it. I can feel it.

I lobbed a grenade aimed low and fired a burst from my carbine as I leaped into hole number three. Hole number three was occupied! I was too close to shoot. Instinct took over as I grabbed my trench knife and begin stabbing. I stabbed again and again and again, and kept on stabbing I don't know how many times into the body of that unknown Japanese soldier.

Christ, he's dead. He must be dead after all that stabbing. Why do I keep stabbing him? Why not just stab one or two or even three times? Maybe I've become a crazed killer, and once I start stabbing I can't stop. What if I get back home and go off my rocker and start stabbing people for no reason? Wait a minute. What if it's not a Jap I just killed? What if it's Carlos or Sullivan? Christ, I might have killed one of them. Now what?

I steeled myself against the possibility that I might have killed a fellow Marine. I muttered to myself, *Semper Fi, Mac, it's my hole. You shouldn't have been here.*

I lay frozen there with those thoughts racing through my mind, my hand still gripping the Kabar knife I had just used on this unknown person. Damn, I had to know. I ran my hand over the body, hoping the best while fearing the worst. He seemed to be small, that's a good sign, but, hell, Carlos was small. I probably killed Carlos.

As I reached for the man's boots I was exhilarated by what I felt; Hobnail boots. Then I knew I had killed a Japanese soldier, not Carlos.

I lay still, not daring to move lest I give away my new position. More crazy thoughts were running through my head. I asked for just five more minutes. I was so goddamned scared I was shaking all over.

I'll probably die of fright. How is that going to look on my tombstone?

HERE LIES DENNIS OLSON
FIGHTING MARINE
"DIED OF FRIGHT"

Maybe I'll last another five minutes if I just lie quietly. Hope I don't go to sleep and snore and give my position away. What the hell is that smell? Oh yeah, it's that guy I just killed. He lost control. Happens almost every time someone gets killed. Christ, I wish I could get him out of my hole; I can't stand the smell. That's the worst part of this goddamn war- the smell…well, maybe not the worst but it ranks up there pretty high. I never get used to it. I wish that fucking captain what's his name on Tarawa had a good taste of some of this shit so he could know what this war is all about. I'll never get over the way that sonofabitch treated us. I hope the bastard dies with a hard-on. If I die, Johnson and Williams will be ticked off. I owe each of them twenty bucks. Should've told them to collect from Amellio; he still owes me a hundred. No big deal. They're probably all dead by now.

Suddenly I heard a faint swishing sound. What the hell is it? It's close—too close. It might be a Mamba snake. They live on this rat hole of an island. I saw a guy get bit by one. Fell on him as he walked under a tree while on patrol. He was dead before we could get him to a corpsman.

It'll be just my luck to get killed by a fucking snake. Damn, I hate snakes! What the hell is it? Come on ears, eyes, nose, brain. Let's work together on this. Oh hell, it's just the chin-strap on my helmet swinging in the breeze. Christ, now I know I'm going crazy. How could I mistake a chin-strap for a Mamba? Wonder how many got killed tonight. There's been a lot of shooting up and down our perimeter. Seventeen went on watch at dusk. How many will be alive at dawn? Two weeks ago we had fifty-three men: Twenty-nine killed before tonight; the rest wounded or down with malaria or dengue fever.

Without thinking I reached for a cigarette and was about to flick my Zippo when I caught myself.

Might as well smoke, my five minutes were up a long time ago. This is as bad as it's going to get. Nothing will ever measure up to this. I said that when I waded ashore at Tarawa. I wish this war would end. I sure as hell didn't know it was going to be this bad. All that crap they fed us in training about how invincible a well-trained fighting Marine is was pure bullshit. Hell we're no more invincible then anyone. I learned that on the landing boat at Tarawa when I saw Lieutenant Jacobs take a fifty to his face. What a bloody mess that was. Splattered blood on everyone near him. The sight of that shocked us all. We were all new to this killing game and though we were trained for it we weren't prepared for it. Then Sergeant Corona ordered the ramp dropped and everyone near the bow got killed, even Corona. If anyone was invincible it was him. He was all Marine; a gung-ho hard-nosed sonofabitch; lived through the whole damn Guadalcanal campaign, but when that ramp went down so did Corona.

That was my last conscious thought in the foxhole.

CHAPTER 34

THE HOSPITAL SHIP

Lying on my back I could see daylight through the slits of my half-open eyes. I wondered where I was.

A form came into view; the form of a beautiful woman, as near as I could tell. I tried to focus, but thinking I was dreaming, fell back asleep. I was startled to hear a voice—a woman's voice. That got my attention, and my eyes snapped open. Leaning over me was that woman trying to shake me awake. My first thought was that I had died and gone to heaven, but she was saying something: What was she saying? My head cleared and I realized she was yelling in my face.

"You are on a Naval hospital ship; you have been sleeping for two days. It's time for you to wake up."

What a shock. How did I get here. Have I been wounded?

I did a quick but complete examination of all my body parts to make sure they were where they belonged. I was more than just a little gratified to know everything was OK.

A Navy mess-cook brought me a tray of food—real food, not K-rations or any of that kind of crap. Looked like typical stateside Navy chow: Swiss steak, mashed potatoes, canned vegetables and Jello. Big mug of coffee, and a couple cigarettes.

Damn, it don't get no better than this. If this is a dream, it sure is a good one. I must have been as filthy as a pig when I came in here. Someone cleaned me up and put this nightshirt on me that doesn't close in the back. I wonder if the nurse who woke me up did that. Too bad I was asleep. The mess cook is talking to me but I can't hear him. Christ, I'm deaf!

I can't hear a damn thing he's saying. Wait a minute…I heard the nurse, but she was yelling. Hope it's not going to be permanent. If I live through this fucking war, I damn sure don't want to be deaf for the rest of my life. I don't want to be blind, either. I sure as hell don't want to be crippled, with a fake leg, or a fake arm. But mostly I don't want to be paralyzed from the neck down or even from the waist down and paddle around in a damn wheelchair. If I live through all these battles and am lucky enough to go home, which probably isn't going to happen anyway, but if I am lucky and go home I want to be in one piece, not all fucked up. I want to be able to do all the things I did before. If I can't do that, then I don't want to go back.

I had no recollection of the last minutes in the foxhole. I supposed a grenade had landed too close, but I would have to learn the details when I returned to my unit. I knew any dreams of transfer stateside or to Hawaii wouldn't come true since, miraculous as it was, I couldn't find any physical damage. Certainly my bell was rung in the foxhole that night, but that didn't count. The hospital staff was monitoring my hearing loss, and my ability to hear was improving daily, and after about ten days was near normal.

Without doubt I was the least damaged of all those in my ward. Some were horribly wounded; bandaged over large parts of their bodies; some with arms or legs missing; a few seemingly not wounded at all, but maybe they were the most damaged. Their blank stares and expressionless faces reminded me of the dead Marines and Japanese soldiers I had seen so many of these several months last past, while in the midst of this hell, called war.

CHAPTER 35

THE PAST AND THE FUTURE

I was discharged from the hospital ship and transported to shore by way of a Higgins boat. A jeep was waiting to transport me and two others back to the airfield headquarters to rejoin our platoon. I recognized the driver as Sergeant Bost from the Tarawa campaign. It was good to see a friendly face, and we greeted each other warmly.

"How ya doing, Big Hoss? I heard you got knocked on your ass on security watch. You about ready to get back to some more of that shit?"

"Hell yes. I never get enough of security watch. I'm just sorry I had to stay on that fucking hospital ship so long. I had to eat real Navy chow and lay around checking out the nurses and seeing a movie every night. It was tough duty, and I'm glad it's over with. How the hell you been Bost? I haven't seen you since Tarawa."

"Not too bad. We got a new platoon leader, a real odd duck, and I'm still trying to figure him out. He came in with the replacements. I hear they got their asses kicked at Naha."

"Hell, that's where I was, me and my buddy Reznik. They kept us on the line so long we almost all got killed. I was sure glad to see them new guys."

"Where's Reznik? Did he buy it?"

"Naw, it's a long story. I'll tell you later."

Bost dropped me off in front of battalion headquarters, one of the few buildings at the airfield not completely destroyed. I identified myself to a clerk near the entrance and asked who my new platoon leader was and where I might find him. I was told to report to 1st Lieutenant Bernstein, down the hall to the right.

"Thanks, Mac," I muttered to the clerk.

How could I be so damned unlucky as to get hooked up with that guy again? I thought I saw the last of him at Guam. First Lieutenant? He was Second Lieutenant at Guam. What could he have done to get promoted? I didn't know stupidity got rewarded out here, but it doesn't surprise me either.

"Corporal Olson reporting for duty, sir."

"Don't you believe in knocking, Corporal?" The lieutenant asked without looking up.

"On what, the wall? I don't see a door to knock on," I answered with as much sarcasm as I could muster, only then noticing the lack of a wall behind Bernstein. "to say nothing of a missing wall. You must rate pretty high around here, Lieutenant."

Bernstein, ignoring my remark, said, "I've been looking over your service jacket, Olson. Looks like you've been busy since you left Guam. Let's see. Got your bell rung passing ammo on the LST, rescued the Army at Naha, lost almost your whole company before we relieved you, sent back here to guard the airfield, had some damn rough dusk-to-dawn security watches, Almost ate a Jap grenade. Christ, what didn't you do, Olson? Trying to win the war by yourself?"

I was taken aback by a note of understanding in Bernstein's words. Maybe he had learned something about the war since that day he had us lined up, chewing ass at Guam. It wouldn't have surprised me if someone had fragged his ass after that session.

In answer to his question, I said, "Sir, this has been no better or no worse than it was at Tarawa. What the hell do you think we been doing out here? You think all we do is get drunk on fermented prunes? What do you think First Sergeant O'Reilly was trying to tell you there at Guam?"

"We all learn, Olson, and I learned a lot when we relieved your company at Naha. We truly did get a taste of what it was all about, like First Sergeant O'Rielly tried to point out to me at Guam.

Report to Sergeant Bost for a new tent assignment. Best of luck to you, Olson. I hope you make it through the rest of the war."

"Thank you, sir," I answered, this time without sarcasm.

"One more thing, Olson. I was told to pass some information along to you. Your buddy, Louis Reznik, is in the hospital at Pearl."

"Thanks again, Lieutenant."

I already knew that, but thanks anyway, I muttered to myself.

I was anxious to see my new digs and was looking forward to a nice, pyramidal tent, with a sand floor, where fleas thrive. I was hoping for one without sides so I could get good air circulation. I ran into Pop Schuber on Main Street. He seemed genuinely glad to see me, but you could never tell about Pop.

"How ya' doing, Olson? Bost said you was back. Guess you're gonna be in with me and some of the old salts from the Tarawa and Guam campaigns."

"Well, that's great, Pop. I'm looking forward to it. Maybe we can get up some serious games. I always enjoyed playing poker with you."

"I'm glad to hear that, Olson. It gave me great pleasure separating you from your money. You were a good loser, and I respected you for that; still do."

There it was—the old square needle, which he used often and effectively. I got a kick out of the "kiss-my-ass" exchange I always had with him, and I think he did too.

"Pop, you remember when we bivouacked at the tomb and Charlie spotted us and you and Cleat hit the entrance at the same time and got stuck?"

"Yeah, I remember. What about it?"

"You remember my little Brownie camera?"

"Of course I do. What are you getting at, Olson?"

"When you and Cleat were stuck, I snapped a couple pictures of you, and I thought I'd send them to your girl friend in Texas. You wouldn't have a problem with that, would you, Pop?"

"You do and I'll kick your ass big time."

"That'll be the day. By the way, Pop, where's that wonderful tent you been bragging about?"

"Find it yourself, ass-hole."

I first met Pop when we were in the same platoon, walking all over Okinawa, looking for the main Japanese forces. He and Father Cleat were a two-man bazooka team and argued constantly about who was supposed to carry which part of the weapon. Father Cleat, the smaller man, was stuck toting the tripod, the heaviest part; but that's not the only thing they fought about. It didn't take much to get them started and it seemed they argued constantly about anything and everything. However, they had one thing in common. They both had stomach problems, which they complained about endlessly. It was like they were always trying to outdo each other describing the pain and misery they were suffering. Tums were an important part of mail call for them both, and about the only time they had kind words toward each other was over Tums. If one didn't receive any at mail call and the other did, they shared equally. If neither received any, they were back at each other fighting about everything. Father Cleat was twenty-seven and Pop Schuber was twenty-six. Most of us were in our early twenties, with the iron constitution of youth, and could eat most anything. Neither of them enjoyed that luxury.

I knew I had been successful getting under Pop's skin, and could look forward to some lively exchanges. It was one way of passing time between battles. Another was playing poker, but my all time favorite was getting drunk, which wasn't hard to do on that flea-infested island. The only good thing I could say about Okinawa was that sake was quite easy to come by, and I intended to come by some as soon as I got squared away. Sake wouldn't have been my first choice if I had a choice, but since I didn't have a choice I drank it and was damn glad to get it. It had a very good numbing aspect to it, with none of the disastrous effects of the fermented prune wine we drank at Guam.

I located my new quarters and found Kurth on his bunk, thumbing through the same dog-eared, beat up girlie magazine I remember seeing on Guam.

He jumped up and began pumping my hand. How you doing, Olson? I heard you was back from the hospital ship."

"I'm good, Kurth. How you been? You still pulling all-nighters?"

"Hell yes. Since the fighting stopped down south it's worse than ever for us here at the airfield. The Japs are fragmented and don't have the power for an outright assault but they try to overrun our lines every night. It's just like the night you got nailed and went to the hospital ship."

"Kurth, I don't know what happened that night. The last thing I remember was Japs coming at me. I remember throwing a grenade in their direction. That was it. Next thing was waking up on the hospital ship. Maybe you can fill me in."

"Well, yeah—maybe—It was pretty confusing that night. I was in a hole about fifteen yards from you and a little ways to your rear, which is probably why you were the first one the Japs hit. There was some shooting up and down the line, some from your location, then nothing for about thirty minutes. All of a sudden Jap grenades began coming our way, a lot of grenades. I think that's when your lights went out. We got help from some of our guys and drove them back into the boondocks where they came from. When it got light we counted our losses, one of which was you. I thought you was dead; you sure looked dead. You had been thrown about three yards from your foxhole. Funny thing, though, Olson, when we found you, a dead Jap was lying across you, covering part of your body. He had a knife stuck in his chest. We never could figure out what that was all about."

"How many of our guys got killed that night, do you know?"

"Four killed and three wounded. I didn't know any of them. They were all replacements. I try not to get acquainted with any of the new guys."

"About the Jap with the knife in his chest, Kurth, that was my knife, and I put it there. In that first skirmish, about thirty minutes before the main attack, I vacated one hole and jumped into another one. That guy was already there, and I got him before he could get me; hacked him up real good with my knife."

"Olson, the way you and him was all tangled up it was kinda hard to figure out, but it sure looked like if he hadn't been there, sprawled all over you like he was, you would've got killed. He was a mess; his guts were hanging out, and his head was almost blown plum off."

After a long pause I said, "This whole thing is kinda' spooking me out. Isn't it about chow time? Let's go hit the line."

Later that night I got re-acquainted with my new tent mates, and after the usual exchange of platitudes, conversation turned serious. There was a strong line of camaraderie drawing us together as we had all been through the battles at Tarawa or Gualcanal, and Guam and here at Okinawa. There was a common feeling of concern about whether we would live through another battle.

Castana put it like this. "The way I see it, I only got so many chances at staying alive against the odds of getting killed. I been in so damn many battles without getting hit I think my luck must be about run out."

Pop Schuber said, "Shit, Castana just keep doing what you're doing and you'll probably live through it all. I think you'll make it, too, Olson. You're probably too stupid to get killed."

"Well, if I'm too stupid to get killed, what do you think keeps you alive?"

That shut him up, but probably not for long.

Kurth seemed genuinely concerned about living through more action. He said, "I agree with what Castana just said. Luck is going to keep you alive just so long before it runs out. Every time I do a dusk-to-dawn watch I think it'll be my last."

Riley said, "I think when your time's up it's up and you can't do nothn about it one way or another, so it doesn't do any good to worry about it."

Bost said. "You might be right, Riley, but I for one don't buy into that shit and I don't think you do either. Are you saying when your time is up it's up and you don't need to worry about getting hit and you can leave your foxhole when you get bored and just wander over to visit with your buddies?"

"Hell no! That's stupid. I didn't say that at all. You have to take care of your ass all the time, stay down and cover up and do all the shit you need to do to stay alive. Beyond that there ain't nothin you can do, it's out of your hands."

"Well whose hands do you think it's in?" Bost asked.

"Me, personally, Are you asking me whose hands I think it's in?"

"Yeah, I guess that's what I'm asking you."

"Bost, you're pinning me down big time here, but since you put it that way, I guess I gotta say I think it's in God's hands. I know something a lot bigger than luck keeps me alive, and I figure it must be God."

"I don't mean to shatter your belief system, but I think staying alive or getting killed is shit-house luck, and I think I can prove it."

Bost proceeded with what he considered to be the proof to support his statement.

"I remember on the first day of fighting at Tarawa, when everything was all fucked up and no one knew what to do, some of us were forming up behind one of our tanks to advance on the enemy. Lieutenant Sizemore was in command. I bent down to pick up my Browning, which I had dropped when a mortar landed real close. In the split second it took me to pick up my weapon, Lieutenant Sizemore was hit and instantly killed by a shot fired from a trap door foxhole behind us. Now that ain't no big deal by itself because a lot of guys were getting hit, but what made it a big deal for me was, if I hadn't bent over at just that instant, that shot would have killed me instead of Sizemore."

"So what are you saying, Bost?" Riley asked.

"What I'm saying is, the simple but timely act of bending over is what saved my ass. It was a matter of shit-house luck, pure and simple. Good luck for me, bad luck for the lieutenant."

"How do you know it was luck and not God saving your ass?" Riley asked.

"Well, shit, Riley, I don't know if it was God or shit-house luck. It's just the way I see it."

Riley, not convinced by Bost's argument, said, "I think your 'shit-house luck' theory is pure bullshit. I think God saved your ass, and I think you do too."

"Well there you go, Riley. You think your way, and I'll think my way."

"Works for me, Dude."

"What worries me," Castana said, "is the rumors I been hearing about invading Japan. Now that just scares the crap right outa me. I don't want no part of that, and I think we earned our right to miss out on that one."

I thought Schuber had drifted off to sleep, but all of a sudden he came alive.

"Do you guys realize the Air Corps rotates the bomber crews back home after a certain number of combat flights?" Not waiting for an answer, he continued, "My kid brother was a gunner on a B-26, flying missions outa' England, and when they completed twenty, they sent 'em back home."

Riley, with a similar story to relate, said, "My best friend from high school was on a cruiser, and they was in the Corral Sea Naval battle, and they did some other stuff, too, but anyway, when they went back to the States to get their ship patched up, he got reassigned and was sent to school in Chicago."

Pop Schuber said. "So that's just my point. Everybody else gets rotated back home except us jarheads. How come we ain't included in that rotation shit?"

Carlos, who never had much to say, in a way said what we were all thinking. "I don't think none of us is going back alive. I think that as long as we ain't dead yet they're gonna keep sending us into these battles. They don't give a shit if you live or die. If you live, they send you to the next battle. If you die they bury your ass and send someone in to take your place. They don't give a shit who they send in to the next battle or who they bury. If they did they wouldn't just keep sending us from one battle to the next, with dusk-to-dawn security watches in between. It's like they know fucking well we're gonna get killed eventually. The way I see it is the next battle will wipe us all out, and the next battle is Japan."

His words were profound, and I think they struck a cord with everyone. For once Pop was quiet, staring off into space. Riley started to speak but changed his mind.

Castana was the first to speak up. "Carlos, it's goddamn hard to argue with what you just said. We keep losing more people all the time, and they just send us more guys to take their place. It's just a matter of time before each one of us will be the one they replace."

Pop got up and walked out, saying, "I'm gonna go find Cleat and get drunk."

"That's one of the smartest things you ever said, Pop. Anyone got a bottle of Sake?" I asked.

Kurth reached under his bunk and pulled out a bottle. No one wasted time breaking out his tin cup.

CHAPTER 36

WHATS OUT THERE?

It didn't take long to get back into the swing. It was the same drill as before my stay on the hospital ship, with security watches every night in a foxhole or a machine gun emplacement, or hunt-and-kill patrols during the day. That tactic was working well for our guys. The Japanese forces were diminishing while we were gaining in strength because our platoon was kept up to strength with new Marines to replace those killed or wounded on security watch or on patrol.

My first security watch after my stay on the hospital ship was the same as all the others. Hillman was in a hole about ten yards to my left, and Carlos was over on the other side.

There wasn't as much enemy action as there had been before I got nailed, but enough to keep us on our toes. The new guys were a pain in the ass. I was damn glad to see them, that's for sure; but they needed to calm down. Every time they heard a noise they got excited and started shooting, making themselves a good target for the Japs, and every time they did that they got shot.

I wonder if the rumors about invading Japan are true. Like Carlos said; none of us will live through that. Christ, I don't want to go there. The way these people defend these worthless damn islands, even when they know they can't win, blows my mind. They'd rather kill themselves than be taken prisoner; I've seen it happen many times, though, I must admit, at times we kill prisoners. It's particularly disturbing here on Okinawa, where there's a civilian population. During the Naha battle, whole families made their way to the cliffs and jumped off together

185

rather than turn themselves over to our forces. The only way that makes sense is if they were pretty damn sure we'd kill them if they surrendered to us, and the only way they could think that way was if their leaders had convinced them of it. They were probably told we were the aggressors and had started the war. Maybe they were told we had bombed their navy in Yokohama Harbor and killed three thousand sailors. Their battle cry was probably, "Remember Yokohama Harbor."

I hope I dug these holes deep enough. I have a bad feeling about tonight. Nothing new about that- I have a bad feeling every time I do a security watch. I always think it's going to be my last. Christ, it's dark; I been here three hours and I still can't see. I hope I'll hear them if they come my way. I heard something a few minutes ago. Maybe I just thought I did, but if I hear it again I'll spray a few rounds their way just to let 'em know I'm here. Yeah, that would be real bright, Dennis- just like the new guys. There it is again; goddamnit, someone's out there. I know it, but I don't know what to do. I better stay low and keep quiet. They don't know I'm here or they would have tossed a grenade my way. Try to play it smart; you've been through worse and you're still alive. Yeah, but I keep hearing stuff going on out there.

I think it must be getting close to dawn. That triggers memories: "Marie, The Dawn is Breaking." I don't see the dawn breaking, if only it would. These all-night watches seem never to end. My eyes are tired from constantly straining to see. I'm tired all over, even my nose and ears feel tired How could that be? Noses and ears don't get tired. Maybe I'm cracking up. A cup of strong coffee would sure taste good right now. Damn, these mosquitoes are driving me nuts, and I know I'll never get used to these fucking fleas. They been with us ever since we hit Okinawa; they're worse in the foxholes, and there's no way to get rid of 'em. They seem to have an armpit fetish. I have to keep my arms close to my sides to keep 'em out. I wish this fucking war was over. Why don't these assholes just give it up? They must know they can't win. They lost every battle since Guadalcanal, and here we are knocking on their front door and they continue fighting. What would happen if they killed us and destroyed the radar we're protecting? What the hell good would that do them? Even if they broke through, the worst they could do would be to knock out one or two of our bombers, and the effect of that would be like a gnat biting a rhinoceros on the butt.

I know they're out there, but where? They don't know where I am either; and I intend to keep it that way. At last, a glimmer of light in the east; dawn at last. I see something. Looks like movement about fifteen yards out. I wish my eyes would focus; it's blurry, but it looks like two men standing upright. That's strange; I've never seen anything like that before. Maybe they're trying to draw fire; but why would they do that? It's too dark to be sure. Maybe my eyes are playing tricks on me. Now I can hear them, and I definitely see movement. Here they come. What to do? Grenades, of course, dummy. Stay calm. One should do it. Fifteen shots from the carbine won't hurt. Into the other hole. Duck down and cover up. Wait for return fire. No return fire? Stay down. Another clip in the carbine. No grenades yet? Wait a couple minutes, then a quick look. It's light enough for them to see me if they look my way. Better stay down a while longer, should be some dead ones out there. Oh crap, what if this is a repeat of the black robe nightmare, only on a small scale? I don't wanna look. What if I just killed monks wearing black robes? That can't be it; there wasn't any screaming. I gotta' know what happened; just a quick peak. What the hell is that black hump out there? I don't remember seeing that last night. I'm going to stay put until it gets lighter. I can't risk going out yet.

Light enough now. The Japs always pull out at first light. Go see the damage, Dennis.

What the hell? It's a mangled damn horse. I killed a fucking horse, thinking it was two Japs. Well that really ties it; I never did anything like that before. I guess nothing escapes this war, even horses.

"What was all the shooting about, Olson?" Shouted Hillman as he ran up to join me. "Is that a horse? Good God almighty, Olson, what the fuck did you do?"

"Well now just what the fuck do you think I did? I killed the sonofabitch because I thought it was two or three Japs closing in on me."

"What did you do, shove a grenade down his throat?"

"Get lost, Hillman; you would've done the same thing. Don't give me no shit about this."

"Damn," I said. "Here comes Carlos; probably gonna give me a ration of crap, like you just did."

When Carlos arrived he stared at the mangled horse for about a minute, then burst out laughing.

Between fits of laughter he said, "Olson is this the way you break horses in North Dakota? I was raised on a ranch in Arizona and I broke a lot of horses, but I never broke one with a grenade. What are you gonna do with him now you got him under control?"

"Carlos, you're about as funny as a dose of clap, so why don't you just go tuck your ass in and go nitie-nite before I rip you a new one."

As he headed toward camp for chow and much-needed sack time he turned and flipped me off. "Up yours, Olson," he said, still laughing his ass off.

A couple nights later, Pop Schuber told me Meatnose Hillman had been killed in his foxhole. He said his throat was cut, and a Jap knife was stuck in his chest. His death bothered me more than any of the others. We had been together since boot camp, and I had become quite fond of him. He was just such a damn decent guy who never had a bad word to say about anyone. He always did his job and did the right thing by everyone. It wasn't possible to dislike him and I was greatly saddened by his death. He didn't deserve to be killed; of course none of the guys deserved to be killed, but in his case it just seemed to hit me harder than the others. I remember thinking how much I hated the war at that time, and how distressed I felt. I needed to take a walk and be alone for a while. I had never felt this bad about any of the other guys getting killed. Hillman was like a little brother who needed to be taken care of, too late for that now. I wanted to cry, but I didn't know how. The great irony for him was that was to have been the last security watch he would have to pull. Well, actually it was his last security watch, but not in a good way.

Goodbye, my brother.

Things were slowing down a lot. There were nights when the enemy didn't show up at all, like the night I killed the horse. We all had the feeling it might be coming to an end. Our lifestyle was definitely improving; chow was better than it had ever been, and we were getting beer, a lot of beer; two bottles a day, and if some candy-ass recruit didn't want his I could buy it from him, and I damn sure did. As a matter of fact, I searched out as many of those types as I could find and paid whatever it took to get their ration. Add to that the fact that those of us who had been out here fighting all those battles had been taken off the foxhole security watches and were getting the easy duty assignments like guard duty at the radar trailer. The new guys were getting the foxhole security watches.

I figured Lieutenant Bernstein was responsible for all of that. There was definitely a change in his attitude toward me when I met him in his office without a wall after my vacation on the hospital ship. I suppose after a week on the battle line where he not only saw men killed and wounded but heard their screams of agony and smelled the smell of death. Experiencing first-hand the gut-wrenching fear of facing the ferocity of battle, might have influenced his thinking. He probably came to realize the spit-and-polish military bullshit takes a back seat to that reality, and that his position was to lead men in battle, not to sustain that grand allusion. The main thing is he didn't have to do anything for us; none of the others ever did. I was greatly impressed by that, and I intended to tell him.

I found him in his office without a door or an outside wall, writing letters to the mothers, dads, and wives of those recently killed.

"What can I do for you, Olson?" He asked.

"I figure you've already done it, Lieutenant. Chow is great, and the beer ration is coming through like gang-busters. I just wanted to tell you how much we all appreciate it, though I think I'm the only one who knows who to thank."

"It was the least I could do to square things at Guam. First Sergeant O'Reilly tried his best to clue me in, but unfortunately I couldn't relate to what he was trying to tell me at that time."

"It takes a big man to not only see the truth but to act on it with the conviction you have, and I gotta tell you, Lieutenant, I just admire the hell out of you for that."

"I appreciate your kind words more than I can say, Olson, but the truth of the matter is I see things as either right or wrong, black or white, with little or no gray in between. I don't say that with pride or necessarily as a wise approach, but it is the way I've always viewed things, and it's been the yardstick I've used to guide my life. Perhaps in the future I might develop a less stringent view. Ten days on the Naha line put me in touch with an experience I shall never forget for as long as I live. Seeing young men lose their lives in a most horrible way is a memory that will be with me forever."

Chapter 37

DREAMS

There, behind my bunk, growling menacingly, was a big Bengal tiger. I leaped out of my bunk and yelled to Castana, "Help me kill this sonofabitch before he kills me! I can't find my carbine. Where the fuck is it? It's always right here. Where's my fucking carbine?"

"It's right here," Castana said as he leaped out of his sack, "but damn it, Olson, you don't need it. There's nothing here."

"The hell there isn't. Look behind my bunk at that fucking tiger and tell me there's nothing there."

"Wake up, Olson, you're dreaming. Here, look for yourself. Do you see a tiger? You're having a dream. Shut up and go back to sleep."

That wasn't the first time I dreamed about a tiger at the head of my bunk, and it wasn't the last. I had that dream many times, and it was always exactly the same. The first several times I knew the tiger was there, and I jumped out of my sack looking for my carbine. Of course there never was a tiger behind my bunk; but those dreams were so real it took a long time for me to realize what was happening and to be able to get a handle on the situation. Another troublesome dream I had on a regular basis was of a black-hooded skeleton walking toward me, smiling. As it approached to about two yards of me it just faded away. As weird as it sounds, I didn't feel threatened by it, though I should have, being as gruesome as it looked.

I'm not the only one who had dreams. A marine from another tent had a habit of running through the company area, yelling, "Bonsai; mock-a-hi, kill 'em all, kill 'em all."

No one knew who he was, and we all just went back to sleep, figuring he was harmless, until one night he ran into a tent yelling the bonsai thing and attacked one of the guys with his bayonet. He didn't stab him; he just used it as you would a club, and fortunately the guy was able roll away after receiving one blow from the flat side of the blade. The bayonet-wielding nut-case was out of the tent before anyone was able to identify him, and the question became, "What the hell do we do now?" The guy was obviously dangerous, and we needed to do something about him. I slept with my .45 in my hand, with a shell in the chamber. I figured if he yelled first I might wake up in time to get a shot off before he hacked me up. It became a real problem when he attacked guys two nights in a row, using not the flat side but rather the stabbing end, seriously injuring them both. We never could figure out what to do about "Bonsai Guy," which became his moniker. It was a running joke to greet someone the next day and ask, "Are you Bonsai Guy?" Then he quit coming around and speculation was he got killed or wounded in a foxhole or on patrol, and none of us felt remorseful about that. It was just a great relief to not have that ass-hole to deal with anymore. It was bad enough worrying about whether you were going to live through another night in a foxhole or come back alive from a "hunt-and-kill" patrol without agonizing about your own people hacking you up.

Another guy a few tents away used to wake up screaming the most godawful screaming you ever heard. He was so damn loud he probably scared away any Japs who might have been close by. He seemed harmless, unlike Bonsai Guy, and of course we all knew who he was. His name soon became "Screamer," and he was never able to live down that name. Worst of all, he never did quit screaming. Joe Blow, no kidding, that was his name, had a habit of getting out of his bunk, dressing, and walking through the company area. The Corporal of the Guard stopped him one night, woke him up and asked where he was going. He said he was going to the corner to get a paper. Another time he almost got himself killed by the sentry at the radar trailer.

"Halt!" bellowed the guard. "Who goes there?"

"Advance to be recgonized."

Joe advanced but he didn't halt. The sentry fired a shot over his head, which fortunately woke him up. The next shot would probably have killed him.

Van Hooten had them all beat for the scariest, creepiest dream. His was about black widow spiders he thought were crawling onto his cot and getting under his blanket. His reaction was always the same. His leaped out of his bunk, frantically running in a circle while brushing the imaginary spiders off. After he had wakened everyone in his tent, and they convinced him it was only a dream, he went back to bed minus a properly erected mosquito net. That dream was so realistic for him he often relived it the following day. At any time or any place he went through the drill of brushing imaginary spiders from his face and head. I felt sorry for the poor bastard. I could see myself having a dream like that, and I think it would have been awful. I was glad my dream was just of a tiger about to tear me limb from limb or of a black hooded skeleton smiling at me.

During the day we all seemed normal, except Van Hooten, but during the night it was a different story. I think everyone had weird, sometimes dangerous dreams. You never knew when you might be the victim or imaginary enemy in someone's whacked- out mind. I'm sure these dreams were brought on by our night-marish existence, where we never knew from one day to the next when we would die— not if, but when. It was never a matter of "if" for me because I knew I wasn't going to live through the war. The thing that puzzled me about the dreams was how come I dreamed about a tiger at the head of my cot, instead of lying on my back looking into the eyes of a snarling Japanese soldier holding a knife with a ten-inch blade over his head, about to plunge it into my face. That kind of a dream would have made more sense. Maybe a professional in matters of the mind could explain it.

As bad as the dreams were, what happened to Leroy Simpson was worse. Leroy was one of the recruits we had trained for combat at Guam. He was a clean-cut candy-assed type who looked to be about sixteen years old. He had a girl-friend back home in Omaha he called Flo. Her name was Florence, and she wrote him regularly. He usually got a bundle of letters from her, and I believe he answered them all. He was really whacked out in love with her and was more than happy to show anyone and everyone her picture. Then the letters quit coming, and after a few mail calls he received a 'Dear John' letter, which, incidentally, everyone ultimately received.

That poor bastard was absolutely devastated, and his personality changed overnight. He became a loner, not wanting to talk to anyone, and was even caught crying when he thought no one was around. He often disappeared for hours, going into areas known to be populated by Japanese soldiers, stalking and killing whenever he could. He cut an ear off every Jap soldier he killed, and that's how it became known what he was doing. He kept the ears in a small ditty bag normally used for shaving gear. The ears begin smelling, and one of his tent mates followed his nose to the source and disposed of the ears posthaste. After losing his ear collection he became absolutely vicious and swore if he ever learned who had taken his treasure he would slice his throat, cut off both ears, and shove them down his victim's throat.

On the first night of the next patrol he went on, he was found dead in his bedroll with his throat cut. A Jap knife lay next to him. It was assumed a lone Jap soldier had slipped into camp and done the deed. That was the official assumption, but reality argued against that. No one else was harmed, and no one saw the lone Japanese soldier, including the posted security guards.

CHAPTER 38

THE LAST HAND

Poker was the pastime of choice, and a game could be found almost any time. The size of the game depended on which side of payday it was. Before payday the games were small, but after payday they became quite large. Fifty-cent ante and table stakes, which meant you could only bet the value of the pot. The pots could become quite large, sometimes over a hundred dollars.

There was one particularly obnoxious sonofabitch in our platoon named Jensen. He was older than most of us—about twenty-six, or twenty-eight. No one liked him, liked him, hell, we hated him. He had a habit of using a particular phrase that was irritating to us all. Every time he was going to do something, like for instance raise the bet, he always started by saying, "Tell you what I'm gonna do." He knew it was annoying, and that seemed to inspire him to carry it to exasperating ends. No one wanted him in the game, and we did everything we could to keep him out. It was well known by everyone in the platoon that Jensen always took his weapon with him when he joined a game and refused to part with it. Kurth suggested we establish a set of rules, one of which disallowed weapons. He figured that would give us the leverage to keep him out of our games. We agreed that was sound logic and settled on what we thought would be effective, and had the company clerk type them up, then posted them in our tent:

Cash only.

No yen or sen notes allowed, unless they're bundled in one-dollar amounts.

Side arms, carbines, or hand grenades cannot be brought to the table.

No wild games. Draw, jacks or better to open, five-card, or seven-card stud. Period!

Our games were usually quite orderly, until Jensen started coming around, and pissing everyone off. We were going to kick his ass out the next time he came around but Pop Schuber had something to say about that.

When Pop Schuber read the rules he came undone.

"I tried to tell you ass-holes not to write up a bunch of fucking rules, but no, you thought you knew it all. Now what're you gonna do? As long as Jensen don't break none of your dumb-ass rules, you can't kick his ass out."

"We figured he wouldn't play if he couldn't carry his piece," Kurth said.

"Well, you probably figured wrong. "He could have it tucked away in his field jacket and you'd never know it was there till he pulled it out and stuck it up your nose."

Schuber always thought he was smart and we were all stupid just because he was older. Actually, I always thought he was a pretty stupid shit, but in that case I had to admit he was probably right. As long as we made and posted the rules, we would have to play by them. Otherwise, why have 'em?

Bost agreed with Schuber that we couldn't keep Jensen out unless he broke the rules, but was quick to remind him about the shit that went down a few days before in one of the other tents.

"You remember how Jones got pissed when Foster bluffed him out of a winning hand with a pair of deuces, and pulled his .45 on him? Shit, I think if Foster hadn't dove out of the tent before Jones had a chance to get a clear shot, Foster would be an ex-person now, and Jones would be on his way home in irons."

Schuber said, "Yeah, and that's another thing. If these guys don't know the game, they shouldn't be in it."

"That's not the point, Schuber," Bost said. "The point is if them guys would've had some rules like we got, Jones wouldn't have had his piece on him. They could have had a 'kiss my ass' exchange, or even duked it out and it would be all over with."

We decided to leave the rules alone, even if they probably wouldn't keep Jensen out. Maybe the problem would resolve itself. Maybe a Jap would toss a grenade in Jensen's hole some night, or maybe one of us might.

A week later we had a friendly game going. Payday was still a few days away so it was a small game, just something to help pass the time. Guess who strolled in? That's right, Mister ass-hole himself.

"I count five players," he said, "so I'm gonna join you turkeys in a very unfriendly game of cutthroat. That is if no one objects, and I don't think anyone does. Right, gentlemen?"

Castana spoke up, saying, "Not right, ass-hole, not as long as you got that cannon strapped on your hip. You know our rules. No firearms allowed."

"Oh yeah, I remember now—you guys are the ones with the pussy rules. OK, here it is, and I better get it back after I win all your money."

About an hour into the game Jensen got cute and was holding up the play. Riley was dealing a hand of seven card stud and everyone had received their first five cards; the first two were face down, called hole cards, and the next three were dealt face up. A round of betting had taken place after each up card was dealt. The betting was light, so everyone stayed in, hoping to improve their hand on the cheap. The sixth card was dealt face up, giving Jensen a pair of sevens. I had a pair of threes, the only other pair showing. Jensen just sat there with a stupid grin on his face, staring at first one person then at another.

"Come on, Jensen, bet or fold," Riley said. "You're holding up the game."

"Tell you what I'm gonna do," Jensen said as he slowly counted a pile of sen notes.

"Damn it, Jensen," Kurth snapped, "you can't use the sen notes unless they're bundled. They're only worth a cent, and it takes forever to count 'em and it holds up the play. Can't you get that through your thick head?"

"Tell you what I'm gonna do," Jensen drawled, ignoring Kurth. He enjoyed the annoyance he was causing the other players. "I got a pair of sevens showing. It's gonna cost you turkeys to stay in this hand."

Riley was getting sore. "Come on an' bet, damn it. From now on, bundle up them sen notes in at least one-dollar bunches or leave 'em out of the game. And another thing. We been hearing you spout off, 'Tell you what I'm gonna do' ever since we been here at Okinawa, and I'm damn tired of hearing it, so knock it off."

"Tell you what I'm gonna do," Jensen continued.

"Damn it, do it," Castana said, "instead of telling us what you're gonna do. Can't that two-bit brain of yours come up with something else to say? Bet."

"Tell you what I'm gonna do. I got three hundred sen here. It's gonna cost ya' three bucks to see the last card."

Everyone called, until it got around to Castana. "I'm gonna bump it four bucks, and no single sen or yen notes will be allowed."

"Bullshit!" shouted Jensen. "All I got is sen and yen bills."

"Well, drop out and bundle 'em up," Riley demanded. "Better yet, drop out and stay out."

"Fuck you!" Jensen roared. "I got money in the pot, and I'm gonna play this hand out."

"Ok," Schorman, a player from another tent, said. "you can 'go light' on the bets and settle up after the hand if you lose."

Schorman, looking around the table, said, "You guys agree to let Jensen go light this hand?"

We all agreed, and Jensen called the four-dollar raise without comment, probably figuring he was going to win. His pair of sevens was the best hand showing, so he controlled the betting. Everyone except Riley stayed in for the four-dollar raise, then dealt the seventh and last card face down.

Jensen broke out in a big smile, and it wasn't hard to figure he'd caught another seven or improved his hand in some other way. In seven card stud it was hard to read the other guy's hand. He could have four sevens—no, he couldn't, Castana had a seven showing; but he could have three sevens or he could have another pair to go with his sevens or he could have a full boat, three sevens and another pair to go with his sevens. A full house is a powerful hand, very hard to beat.

I didn't have shit, just a lousy pair of threes, but he didn't know that. The possibilities of my hand were the same as for his.

"Tell ya' what I'm—" he started to say.

"Knock off that crap or I'm gonna feed you a knuckle sandwich!" Barked Castana as he jumped up and headed around the table. A couple guys grabbed him before he could get to Jensen.

Jensen jerked back and stared up at Castana, a stupid grin on his face, seemingly unfazed by Castana's outburst. "I'm gonna bet a hundred bucks."

"You dumb bastard; you can't bet a hundred," Kurth said. "This is a pot-limit game, and there's not that much in the pot."

I had a plan to put this guy in his place once and for all. I figured a hundred dollar bet would run everyone out except me.

"Let him bet," I said. "Put your cash on the table if you're gonna bet, Jensen. We're damn sure not gonna let ya' go light for that kinda' money."

"I don't have cash, but I can bet my Jap pistol; it's worth a hundred bucks," he said.

"Hell yes, bet your pistol," I said. "Go get it."

"I don't need to go get it; I got it right here," he said as he pulled it out of a pocket in his field jacket.

"What the hell is this all about, Jensen?" shouted Kurth. "You know damn well we don't allow no firearms at our games. From now on you stay the hell out of our games, and out of our tent."

"I'll second that," said Castana.

"Olson, you said I could bet my pistol, so I bet one hundred dollars." he said as he laid his pistol on the table.

Schoreman and Kurth, the players to Jensen's left dropped out. I was to the left of Kurth and it was up to me to call the bet, drop out, or raise the bet. It was time to put my plan into action. I knew he had been losing big time the last couple weeks, and I figured he was broke. Well, now I knew he was or he would have put up cash instead of his Jap pistol.

"Ok, I call your hundred-dollar bet," I said as I counted out five twenties and put them in the pot. "And I raise you two hundred dollars."

Jensen froze. It was obvious he hadn't considered the possibility of anyone calling his bet, much less raising him. He was badly shaken and asked with a noticeable quiver in his voice, "How can I call?"

"Well, shit, Jensen it's not up to you to do anything yet," I answered, "because there's a player before you who needs to declare what he wants to do."

Castana dropped out. It was now up to Jensen.

"Ok, smart ass, you asked how you can call," I said. "you can call with two hundred bucks, or another pistol, or a Samurai, or anything else you have that I think is worth two hundred dollars. So, now tell me what your gonna do."

"Why can't I just go light in the pot?" Jensen whined.

"Because, you stupid jackass, nobody else called your bet and my raise. It's only you and me betting, and if you go light in the pot it would be like me extending credit to a deadbeat four-flushing sonofabitch like you, which I have no intention of doing."

Everyone looked at Jensen. He was beat and he knew it. By kicking up the bet with the pistol he had beaten himself.

"Well, smart ass, I'm waiting for you to tell me what you're gonna do," I said, "call or fold."

Jensen didn't like to be beat and he was visibly shaken, then there was the added fact that he was being made a fool of.

He said, "Damn it, Olson, let me see your hand."

"You're looking at a pair of threes, and that's all you're gonna see till you call my raise."

Jensen's face was as white as a sheet, and his hands were shaking. He sat quietly, staring at me, the hatred welling up in him.

"Well, for once I'd like to hear you say it, Jensen. Tell me what you're gonna do," I said.

There was total silence for a moment. I was pretty sure he was going to do something, but I had no idea what. I was returning his stare, trying to get a clue as to what he might do. He dropped his eyes to the center of the table and seemed to be looking at the pile of money, or the Jap pistol, or both. In that split second he grabbed the pistol, taking me completely by surprise. My heart was pounding.

Holy shit, the sonofabitch is gonna shoot me.

I didn't plan my reaction but rather acted out of pure instinct. I grabbed the front edge of my helmet with both hands and, using it as a club, brought it down on the top of his helmet with as much force as I could muster, driving it down over his ears and knocking him out cold. He got off a wild shot, which hit Riley in his hand.

The sound of the shot roused the camp. Marines came running from all directions, wanting to know what was going on. The sound of a Jap pistol is very distinct; not as loud as a .45 or a carbine. I suppose they all were aware of that fact and probably thought the war had been brought into our camp.

None of us wanted the brass to get involved, and Castana's quick thinking seemed to relieve the tension.

He said to those gathered in our tent, "Riley was cleaning his souvenir Jap pistol and it accidentally went off and he shot himself in the hand."

Chapter 39

JENSENS REVENGE

After the area cleared out, Riley took off for sick bay but before he left said, "When that bastard wakes up I'm gonna put a slug in his paw. This hurts like hell. This is the first time I been shot in this fucking war and I been through Tarawa, Guam, and here, and another marine is the one that shoots me, and with a Jap pistol."

He went off to sick bay, mumbling to himself, "Goddamn this hurts like hell."

The blow on his head must have jarred something loose in Jensen's brain. When he woke up he mumbled, "I wanna see what Olson had. What did he have with them threes? Did he have me beat?"

Schoreman said, "What do you mean, Jensen? Olson didn't have nothing but them threes. You had him beat but you couldn't call his raise, and besides, you're the one that wanted to change the rules and bet a hundred bucks. Looks like you outsmarted yourself and lost. What don't you understand about that?"

Jensen said, "He stole my pot. I'm gonna kill the sonofabitch."

Pop Schuber jumped up from his bunk where he had been crapping out and bent down and faced Jensen. "You already tried that, ass-hole and you saw what you got. You better knock off that crap. He's been fighting Japs longer than an amateur like you. They haven't been able to kill him, and you better not try. But if by some miraculous stroke of luck you do kill him, I guarantee, I'll kill your worthless ass."

Life settled back into a normal routine after the excitement of the Jensen affair, but just for a couple days. I had just been relieved after six hours staring at a radar screen and was bone tired. I sat on my bunk to take off my shoes and felt something squirm under the blanket. I leaped up in a frantic attempt to get away. The only thing that could wiggle like that was a snake. I crashed into Carlos' bunk, tearing his mosquito net down and upending his cot. Fortunately he wasn't in it, as he and Castana were on security watch at the radar trailer. Kurth came up fighting, probably thinking we were being attacked. "Don't shoot, Kurth; it's me, Olson. There's a snake in my sack. Put your piece away; it makes me nervous."

"What did you say was in your—?"

He was cut off mid-sentence by Schuber, who jumped from behind his mosquito net with a flashlight in one hand and his .45 in the other.

"What's going on? Is that you, Olson? Why are you walking in a circle? Are you drunk?"

He immediately turned off the flashlight as we were still on strict blackout orders.

"I wish I was," I answered. "There's a snake in my sack."

With that I grabbed my carbine by the barrel and proceeded to pummel my bunk. I pounded the center and all corners, smashing the stock down until I was exhausted and wet with sweat.

"A snake, how the hell did it get there?" Kurth asked.

Schuber said, "Olson, for Christ's sake, are you having another one of your dreams, only instead of a tiger now it's a snake?"

"I wish it was a dream, Pop. Look under my blanket while I cover you with my poncho to keep the light out and tell me if it's a dream."

"Sure enough, Olson, you got yourself a big snake and it looks like a Black Mamba. Must be three feet long and it damn sure ain't no dream."

"I need to have a look, Pop, let me have your flashlight and, here, hold the poncho for me."

It was a bloody, frightening sight. I was shaking all over and having a hard time breathing.

"How did that sonofabitch get there, Dude? Damn, a three-foot-long Mamba. What's going on, Olson?"

"When I sat on my bunk to take off my shoes I felt that thing wiggle under the blanket. It had to be a snake; nothing but a snake could wiggle like that. I freaked out and crashed into Carlos' bunk. If it had been at the foot of my cot I wouldn't have known it was there until I slipped in and shoved my feet right into it. That would have been curtains for me."

Schuber said, "But how the hell did it get there?" Not waiting for an answer, he continued, "He couldn't just crawl in there by himself. Olson, for Christ's sake, somebody must have put that thing in your sack on purpose."

"I think Jensen put it there."

"Christ, Olson, I think you're right; he said he was gonna kill your ass. As a matter of fact, he would've shot you if you hadn't bonked him with your helmet. The question now is, what the hell are we gonna do about it?"

"'We, hell! This is *my* problem, and I know what I'm going to do about it; but I appreciate your support. What *I'm* gonna do about is; I'm gonna kill the sonofabitch!"

"Let's take a walk Olson and talk this situation over."

While walking toward the latrine, Schuber said, "I agree that you have to kill him, because if you don't he'll kill you, that's for sure. What you don't want is, you don't want to get caught. Murder is against the law, last I heard, even out here."

"If you got any bright ideas, I'm willing to listen."

"Ya gotta make it look like an accident. Maybe you could get behind him when he's in a foxhole pulling a dusk-to-dawn, and use your trench knife on him, hack him up pretty good and make it look like a Jap did it. Or maybe you could scare him away from the area, shoot him and leave him for someone else to find."

I thought about these suggestions and said, "I like the idea of scaring him away from the company area and killing him, and I think I know just how to do it."

"What you got in mind, Olson?"

"I'll tell you later."

I bundled up the snake in the bloody blankets and walked over to Jensen's tent. Once inside I pulled back his mosquito net and gently woke him.

"Jensen, Jensen," I cooed. "Wake up; I brought your little friend."

"Wha—wha—who is it?" Jensen muttered, still more asleep than awake. "Wha— what the hell do you want?"

"It's me, Olson, your stud poker buddy; the guy your gonna kill. Are you awake now?"

"Yeah, I'm awake. What the hell are you doing here; what do you want? I thought you was on watch."

"Guess what I found in my sack when I got off watch? Yeah, that's right, Jensen, your little friend. I brought him back to you so you can get better acquainted with him."

"HERE!"

I jammed the bloody blanket in his face.

"KEEP THAT SNAKE AWAY FROM ME!"

He virtually exploded out of his bunk, and ran wildly down the company street all tangled up in his mosquito net. He continued the insane screaming, "KEEP THAT SNAKE AWAY FROM ME! KEEP IT AWAY FROM ME!"

I'm sure anyone who woke up probably thought it was just another whacked-out jarhead having a dream about snakes. I left the dead snake and the bloody blankets on his bunk and took his bedding in exchange. I didn't think I'd have any more trouble from him that night, so I went back to my tent for much-needed sleep.

CHAPTER 40
JENSEN'S DEMISE

Sometime later, the faint sound of a carbine slide bolt chambering a round woke me up. In the early dawn light the silhouette of someone holding a rifle appeared in the tent entrance. The rifle swung around to point at my bunk. I rolled out on the other side of my cot at the very instant the rifle came to life, sending two slugs into my cot where my head had just been. In a split second my assailant ducked under the tent flap and was gone, out of sight into the half-light of the early dawn.

Other Marines burst out of their tents, guns in hand, thinking the Japs had made a surprise attack. Guys fresh out of combat were still jumpy, and the two shots at dawn had flipped a lot of switches. I spotted Jensen in a group of Marines heading into the boondocks, supposedly looking for the attackers. Others were milling about, not knowing exactly what to do.

I figured this would be a good time to double back to my tent, get dressed, and grab my weapons. I could track down Jensen and kill the sonofabitch. Just then Riley showed up, having been released from sickbay.

"What are these guy's doing out there in their skivvies, Olson, are we under attack?"

"Jensen just took a couple shots at me, but the guy's think Japs slipped in. I'm heading out after him as soon as I get dressed and grab my weapons. When I find him, I'm gonna blow him away."

"Like hell you are! His ass is mine! It's open season, and I got a license. I saw him and some other guys head into the boondocks. I'm going after him and settle the score for both of us."

He grabbed his carbine and was gone.

I crawled into my sack for some evermore needed, hopefully uninterrupted, sleep. This time I was successful and slept till late afternoon.

I was hungry enough to eat dirt, so I headed for the mess hall to resolve that problem. With a mess kit full of something that looked almost edible, I sat down to eat.

"Hey, Olson, did you get the word?" Castana shouted from the chow line.

"What word?" I shouted back. "Meet me over by the fifty-caliber and fill me in."

Castana waited his turn in the chow line, then joined me at the gun emplacement.

He said, "The story is, this morning after the Nip squeezed off a couple rounds, Jensen and Riley and some others went after him. Jensen said when they caught up with the Jap they ran into a trap. He had joined up with two more Nips. Riley got gut-shot and Jensen said he thought he was dead. Jensen was shot in his hand and in his leg. He said the Japs got away."

"How did Jensen get back?" I asked.

"He limped back by himself. He's in sick bay now doing sack drill. The doc patched him up," Castana answered.

"Castana, you need to know something. There never was a Jap in our camp. The two shots everyone heard was Jensen shooting at me. Jensen told everyone it was a Jap, or maybe two, and that he was going into the boonies after them. Some of the guys, including Riley, joined him."

"So you think Jensen shot Riley?" Castana asked.

"I think Jensen and Riley shot each other, and Jensen's the only one who knows where Riley is. I'm going to sick bay and have a little talk with Jensen and find out where the body is. Want to help haul him back?"

"Hell yes. While you're talking to Jensen, I'll round up a few of the troops. We might need help finding him." I walked over to sick bay and found Jensen sleeping. I took a quick look around to see if anyone was near, then woke him by jabbing him in his wounded leg. He came up fighting, so I put my hand over his mouth to muffle his shouts of pain.

"I want to know where you left Riley,"

"I don't know; I think the Jap's took him. He was dead when I got away." Jensen whimpered.

"That's a good story, and maybe someone will believe it, but not me. I think it happened like this: I think Riley caught up with you and shot you in the hand, as he set out to do. You got a shot off and hit him in the gut, or somewhere. Riley went down, but shot you in the leg as you were haulin' ass out of there. Now, where is he?"

Jensen turned belligerent and said, "Get the hell out of here! I don't have to tell you shit. If you want Riley's body, go find it. I'm going aboard a hospital ship in the morning, and I won't have to look at your ugly puss again."

I checked to see if anyone was near, then gave him a hard jab in his leg, just to let him know I meant business. I held him down and covered his mouth so he couldn't yell out.

"You're in for a tough night, Jensen. We rounded up the big brother of that little guy you tucked into my sack the other night. Pop Schuber says it's the biggest Mamba he's ever seen, and he's just waiting for me to give him the word to introduce him to you. Gives me the creeps just thinking about it."

"Goddamn it, Olson, I told you I don't know nothin'!"

"I know what you told me Jensen, and I don't believe you. If you want to act dumb, that's OK with me, but when the sun goes down the fun will begin. Before morning you'll wish you had died quick like Riley- that is if he died. You're the only one who knows about that. Your turn is coming up soon."

With that, I got up to leave.

"No, wait, hold on, Olson," he said. "If you promise not to snuff me with the snake, I'll tell you where I think Riley is, at least where he was the last time I saw him."

"OK, you got a deal. We'll go out an' look. It's simple as hell; no Riley tonight, no Jensen tomorrow. Now, where is he?"

"Remember that Okinawan tomb near the burned-out Jap tank? Last time I saw him he was laid out inside the stone wall in front of the tomb."

"He'd better be there."

I covered his mouth and jabbed him in the leg again, a harder jab than the other two.

"That's for trying to shoot me this morning."

I hustled back to my tent, where the others had gathered, ready to head out in search of Riley. We all looked forward to finding him alive, but none of us were holding out much hope. The only exception was Pop Schuber, who had rounded up Cohen, one of the company corpsman, to join us. He had his first-aid gear as well as a fold-up stretcher.

"Damn, Pop, you're smarter than I thought. That was a hell of an idea."

"Olson, I always been smarter than you, and it ain't never gonna be no different. "I always figured you were born with most of your brains up your ass."

"That reminds me of something. You're from Texas, aren't you, Pop?"

"Yeah, that's right, Olson. You got a problem with that?"

"No problem. A little rhyme just came to mind that I thought you might appreciate."

Not waiting for a response, I continued, "I'm from Texas; I'm rough and I'm reckless; I was born in the outhouse, about an hour before breakfast."

"Olson, that was just about the funniest goddamn thing I think I ever heard. Now, if you don't have no more pearls to share, maybe we can get our asses out of here and go find Riley."

When we got to the tomb we found Riley right where Jensen said he'd be.

"Damn, he looks like shit!" Castana said. "What do you think, doc? Is he still alive?"

Cohen bent down, loosened his field jacket, and waved us all to be quiet as he put his ear against Riley's chest. He listened for what seemed a long time, then took Riley's wrist in his hand to get a pulse count.

"He's alive, but just barely. He's lost a lot of blood; help me get some of his clothes off, so I can get to the wound and stop the bleeding."

Cohen patched him up and got some plasma into him, and we put him onto the stretcher, bundled him up as good as we could, and hauled ass back to camp. We got him to sick bay at about dawn. I don't think any of us thought he'd live— he looked that bad.

I looked up Jensen, but he was gone. I asked the corpsman on duty if he knew where he was.

"He pleaded with the doctor to transfer him to a hospital ship last night," the corpsman said. "The doc couldn't or wouldn't arrange it that fast, and no one here saw him leave. There was a missing tin of alcohol, which we figured he took. He's a real nut case, isn't he? I think that guy could easily qualify for a section eight."

I went to Jensen's tent, hoping to catch him there. Starkey, one of Jensen's tent mates, said he heard him come in late, get his weapons, and leave.

I found a note on his bunk, saying, "Tell ya' what I'm gonna do. Like hell I will."

Two day's later, Jensen was found in front of the Okinawan tomb near where we had found Riley. He was dead, and next to him was a half empty tin of 150 proof sick-bay alcohol; enough to kill a platoon if drunk straight.

Bost said, "I guess too much of the cure for snake bite is as deadly as the snake."

"It couldn't happen to a nicer guy," Castana said. "I hated that sonofabitch, and I'm not a damn bit sorry he's dead."

CHAPTER 41

THE MYSTERY IS SOLVED

"What's the scoop on Riley; has anyone heard anything?"

Bost said, "Cohen told me his condition was too unstable to move him to the hospital ship. He said they were doing everything they could, but they didn't hold out much hope."

Castana said, "That don't sound good. I hope to hell he makes it. He don't deserve to die."

"Goddamn it to hell," I said, "another buddy; a good friend; a fine, decent guy—

Pop interrupted, "You're right, Olson. They don't come no better than him, but we don't want to count him out yet, he still might make it."

"Let's hope so. Castana said.

"If he don't make it, I probably won't get the twenty he owes me," Pop said, "not that I care about the money, but twenty bucks is twenty bucks."

"I've heard you say that before, Pop. Do you think everyone owes you money?

"Well shit, Olson, I don't know who owes me and who don't. "I'm always loaning somebody money, and it's usually a twenty."

"That's really bullshit. I remember a while back you kept hounding me to pay you back the twenty I owed you. I never remembered borrowing twenty from you in the first place, but you kept after me, so I thought, what the hell, maybe I just don't remember, so I paid you. Now, thinking back on that whole deal, I know damned well I didn't borrow any money from you."

"Well shit, Olson I'm pretty damn sure you did, but since you seem so sure you didn't, maybe—now damn it, I said *maybe* you didn't. I'll have to think about it some more."

"Think about it, my ass. You owe me twenty bucks and I want it."

"Well shit, Olson, don't get your balls in an uproar. I'll ketch ya payday, OK? Now are you happy?"

"I'll be happy when I have the twenty in my hand. And another thing, how many guys have you pulled that crap on? I'll bet you been pulling that scam ever since we got here."

"Well shit, Olson—"

"Don't 'well shit, Olson' me anymore. If I don't get my twenty back on pay day, I'm gonna punch your lights out."

"Well sh—

Castana interrupted him. "You're like a broken record, Pop; You remind me of Jensen, always saying. "Tell ya' what—

Schuber cut him off before he could finish the sentence, saying, "Shut up, Castana, I don't need none a yer crap."

A light suddenly popped on in my mind. "Castana, what you just started to say answers a huge question for me

"What are you talking about, Olson?"

"Do you guys remember when I went to sick bay on the LST when I fell and bumped my head?"

"Yeah, I remember that," Schuber said, adding, "You always were un-coordinated, weren't you, Olson?"

I ignored his remark because I knew I had punched holes in his ego in the exchange we just had. He was still chastened and was trying to regain the patriarchal status he had always enjoyed.

Kurth, who had been relaxing on his bunk, reading—correction, looking at a girlie magazine, sat up and said, "I remember that, Olson, but you know something? Your buddy Reznik told me some dude cold-cocked you and took your dough."

"Yeah, that's right, Kurth, Reznik told you right. That's what happened, and now I know who did it."

"Well, who was it?" Kurth asked.

"It was that sonofabitch, Jensen,"

"Yeah, right," Schuber said. "There you go again, spouting more of your bullshit. What makes you think it was Jensen? Ain't you got no respect for the deceased?"

"Not for that deceased sonofabitch. Just before my lights went out I remember hearing someone say what sounded to me like, "Tellahut." I been trying to figure out all this time who said that and what it meant, so I'd know who to get even with."

"I don't get it, Olson," Kurth said. "What does 'tellahut' mean?"

"What it means is, 'Tell you what.' I just heard the first of Jensens famous one-liner."

"So, Olson," Schuber said. "Would you have killed Jensen if you knew he was the one that cold-cocked you and took all your bucks?"

"Hell yes. I intended to kill whoever did it. I just didn't know whose ass to kill."

"Let's get this straight, Olson, because I don't think you're bright enough to figure this out without me explaining it to you."

"Ok, old man, explain it."

"If you had known it was Jensen that did it, and if you had killed him, and if you had got caught, you could easy have got the firing squad or at least sent back to the States in chains,"

"Hell yes, Pop. If I had got caught, but hell's bells, I damn sure didn't figure on getting caught. I wouldn't have shot him in front of Lieutenant Bernstein or the company commander, or dropped a grenade in his mess kit, or I wouldn't have shot him in a poker game like he tried to do to me. I wouldn't have done it like that. I would have nailed him while he was on watch and put a knife in his gut, and the Japs would have been blamed. If I didn't do it that way, I'd figure out something else. There were a lot of ways to do it."

"Olson, you probably don't know how lucky you are it worked out like it did. Think about it a minute, Dude. Everything that happened to him was his own fault. Nobody else did shit to him; he did it all to himself. Now you won't have to hassle your conscience."

"I wouldn't have had a problem with my conscience, Pop, but there's still two things that frosts my ass about the whole deal."

"What's that?"

"He died thinking he had gotten away with stealing my money on the ship. I feel cheated. The other thing is, I didn't get the money back the sonofabitch stole from me."

We hadn't heard anything about Riley, so Bost and I went over to sick bay to see how he was doing. One of the corpsmen told us we were too late, that he had died during the night. He'd now be put to rest along with the hundreds of Marines, Army, Navy, and Air Corps personnel who had also lost their lives at a place none of them wanted to be.

Chapter 42

ITS OVER!

Life got easier for us. The enemy was nowhere to be found, and for all intent and purposes the battle was over. Beer, though rationed, was fairly easy to come by in amounts over and above the legal ration, and sake was plentiful. Chow was better than ever.

"It ain't ever gonna get no better than this," Schuber said as we stood in the chow line. "I heard we're getting steak again tonight, and that's the second time this week. What do you think, Olson, are you a happy hombre?"

"Yeah, I'm a happy hombre, and I'm gonna be happier tonight cause I'm gonna get drunker than a motherfucker. Wanta join me, Pop?"

"You kidding? Hell yes, I'll join you."

"I got something special. You're gonna love this."

"What's going on, Olson? Ya' line up some dancing girls?"

"You'll see after the movie."

"What's playing tonight?"

"Same as last night. That silly-ass musical with Frankie dancing around in that stupid-looking sailor suit."

The blackout had been lifted, and we were seeing a movie almost every night, same as on Guam. Everyone turned out, and after the movie the p.a. came on with an announcement:

"THE WAR IS OVER!" The announcer said. He didn't get a chance to continue his statement until the shouting and whistling stopped, then went on with his announcement.

Two bombs had been dropped on two cities in Japan, we were told— not bombs familiar to us, not even blockbusters like they dropped on some of the cities in Germany to end the war in Europe. They were called "atomic bombs," which we had never heard of, but were told they were so powerful one bomb totally destroyed a whole city. Not only that, they described the devastation of something called radiation fallout from the bomb. The area where the bombs were dropped, they said, would be uninhabitable for seventy years, or more. The whole thing was confusing, but the one thing not hard to understand was that those bombs had ended the war. It was over.

After the movie, back at our tent, I broke out a very large bottle of Old Grandad, which I had acquired from the officers' stash.

"How did you manage this, Olson?" Pop asked.

"You don't want to know, Pop; just enjoy it. What do you guys think about them bombs they dropped on Japan?"

"You already know what I think. Anything that ends this fucking war is OK with me." Pop said.

"I disagree," Castana said. "I don't think anything justifies killing that many people, particularly civilians. Think about it for a minute. Everyone in two cities killed, all the children killed and the women and the old people. How would we like to have something like that happen in some city back home? I think it's bullshit, and I don't think we were justified doing it."

"I agree with Pop," Kurth said. "I never figured I'd live through another battle, particularly if it was going to be the 'battle of Japan,' which is exactly what we had to look forward to. The way I see it is, better them than us."

Let me ask you a question, Castana." Pop said. "Do you think the Japs woulda' dropped them bombs on, say, San Francisco or Seattle if they had em?"

Castana hesitated, then said, "Yeah, I think they would, but that don't mean it was OK for *us* to do it. That's just my opinion."

"Opinions are like ass-holes; we all got em." Pop said.

"How about you, Olson, do you think we shoulda wiped out those two cities and killed all them people?" Castana asked.

"What the hell's the difference if they use one bomb for one city, or if they drop a few of them blockbusters to destroy a city and kill all the people, like they did in Germany? Dead is dead, no matter how you cut it. Do I like the idea of killing all those people? Hell no, I don't. Did we start this fucking war? Hell no, we didn't, but we damn sure finished it. If what they're telling us about this atomic bomb is true, maybe the warlords in Japan and the future Hitlers won't be so damned anxious to start another war, particularly if they know their cities could be wiped out in one fell swoop. Wouldn't it be a hoot if we never had another war like this one, ever again, because of them atomic bombs?"

We spent most of the night getting drunk and celebrating the end of the war. I don't think the officers would have been overjoyed sharing their booze with us, but I figured we deserved it. I'm not a thief, so should I have felt guilty about stealing their booze? Hell no, not even a twinge.

For me the idea of living through all those battles and not getting killed was beyond my wildest dreams. I knew at some point I was going to die, I just didn't know when. From the time our landing boat high-centered on the coral reef at Tarawa and seeing all the guys get killed, I knew it was just a matter of time before I also would be counted among their numbers. The idea that the war was over and I wasn't going to die was simply overwhelming, and I was thankful to God beyond any words I could express.

CHAPTER 43

THE WIND BLEW

The war was over, and those of us lucky enough to have survived were waiting for a ship to take us home; a matter of a few days, a week at most, we were told. It was cold, and the tent sides were softly flapping in a light breeze as I hit the sack. I was thankful for having lived through the war and said as much in a silent prayer. I drifted off to sleep with pleasant thoughts of going home, wondering what the future had in store for me.

Sometime during the night a severe wind and cold rain battered the tent. The canvas began flapping and snapping violently as the tent pegs pulled loose. We all dashed out to drive in the stakes and secure the tent. The cold, driving rain stung my skin like little ice darts, and at that moment all I wanted was to get back to my warm dry cot.

I had no sooner crawled back in when a tremendous gust of wind hit and swoosh, the tent was gone. My cot was upended, and I was thrown out and sent tumbling down the company street like a flake of confetti, completely helpless and out of control. I was disoriented in the turbulent blackness, unable to comprehend what was happening, gripped by fear and the thought that this was the way I would die.

I came to an abrupt stop as I slammed into a tree, draped around the trunk. In that moment I was able to collect my thoughts. The feeling of panic persisted as I realized what was happening but didn't know what to do about it. Instinctively I grabbed the tree trunk and hung on while being fiercely pelted by debris. The deafening screeching of the wind and the objects flying through the air convinced me I should work my way around to the lee side to better shelter myself. I locked my arms around the trunk and held on with all my strength. At times the force of the wind lifted me off the ground. I felt the tree begin to yield to the power of the wind, and figured if it went I'd probably be smashed in the branches, so decided to take my chances and let go.

I tumbled and bounced on the ground until I was deposited into some kind of a pit or ditch, not knowing where I was. My new shelter protected me from the full force of the wind, and as I appraised my situation, decided I had tumbled into the garbage dump. I remembered a gun emplacement the Japanese had dug near the garbage dump facing the sea and figured if I could locate it I might find refuge. I groped along the side until I found the entrance.

Inside the cave, my hopes rose. *Maybe I'll ride out this storm and live to go home after all,* I remember thinking. After a few minutes my hopes were shattered as I felt the mud falling from the dirt ceiling, and realized if it caved in I'd be buried. A blob of mud fell on my head. I panicked and desperately scrambled and clawed my way toward the entrance as the whole roof began coming down. I lunged toward the opening, but my leg was stuck in the mud. It took all my strength to pull it out and dive through the entrance just as the cave collapsed behind me.

The debris was flying about, and even in my semi-protected area I was still in danger. As I was thinking what my next move should be, the whole side of the trench started sliding down, carrying me with it. As I flailed about, trying to get my balance, I bumped into another tree. Desperately, I locked my arms around the trunk and hung on for what I knew was my last chance to survive. I knew I was very near to a cliff that dropped off into the ocean. It was the area where so many local residents had made the decision to end their lives by making the long jump to the rocks below. I had no desire to join them and knew it would take every ounce of energy I had to stay alive.

The wind grew stronger and hurled objects large and small onto me and my tree, which shuddered under the barrage. I wondered how long I'd be able to hang on; how long my tree would be able to hang on. My arms ached and throbbed, and fatigue was taking over. I thought of all the desperate situations I had been in, and decided the Okinawa campaign had to be the worst. Thousands had died there. I thought of the irony I found myself in. The war was over, and I had lived through all those battles. I remember being shot, stabbed, bombed, almost drowned twice, and had a too-close encounter with a Mamba snake. I had lived through malaria and dengue fever, and now my life depended on a tree and my ability to hang on to it.

After what seemed an eternity the wind died down as the early morning dawn lightened the sky. It seemed I had survived another battle— this one against mother-nature.

I tried to loosen my grip on the tree, but try as I might I was unable to release my arms. They were locked in place. I felt desperate.

What to do? What if I never am able to pry my arms loose? What if my arms have been damaged beyond repair and will have to be amputated, even if I am lucky enough to be found? Calm down, Dennis. You've been in jams before and always managed to get out, and you're gonna get out of this one too. Relax, concentrate, and say a prayer of thanks for still being alive, and ask for help just one more time.

The main thing was to unlock my fingers, and after that I was able to pull one arm at a time from around the tree. After a time I got to my feet and carefully worked my way around to see how close I had been to the edge of the cliff. It was a straight drop two hundred feet down, and I could see the ocean splashing against huge rocks. A sickening feeling rushed over me as I imagined falling helplessly toward, and smashing into those rocks below. I had done it. I had cheated death once again. Was it just shit-house luck, as Bost had said, or did God answer my prayers? Of course I could never know for sure, but I certainly knew how I felt about it. I desperately needed God's help and I felt strongly that I had gotten it.

I worked my way up to firm ground and saw the devastation of Yonton Airfield. The hangars were completely destroyed, with their sheets of corrugated steel and all manner of debris strewn about. Several planes were on their backs and the control tower was nonexistent. Exhausted, I sat on a log and tried to pull myself together, my head cradled in my arms, resting on my knees. I wondered if I was the only one to live through the horror of the typhoon. As I sat shivering trying to gather my thoughts, someone tapped me on my shoulder. I turned to see the company chaplain standing behind me.

"What's the trouble son, problems at home?" He asked.

I was completely flabbergasted by his words as I stood to face him, wondering if I had heard correctly. I tried to understand how my near-death experience related to his question. Was that guy serious? What kind of a stupid-ass question was that?

There I was, sitting on a log, wet and shivering, in nothing but my skivvie shorts, bleeding and bruised from head to toe, and this guy is asking if I was having trouble at home. I figured he had either received a blow to his head, was in shock, or just plain whacked out. In any event, I didn't want to talk to anyone who was that far out of touch with my reality.

I answered his question as I turned to leave, "No problem at home, sir. Just out for a breath of fresh air. Nice day, eh?"

I figured his preposterous question deserved an equally preposterous answer. It accrued to me that he might have been in shock at that time, not realizing what he was saying. That being the case, I probably should cut him a little slack; not a lot, just a little.

I staggered toward what was left of the company area, hoping to find a corpsman to treat my injuries. I was exhausted, hungry, thirsty, and shivering from the cold, and just beginning to feel the pain of all my injuries and aching muscles.

The company area was completely destroyed, but emergency facilities were already being set up to take care of the injured. A corpsman gave me a shot of morphine and handed me a blanket and a hot cup of coffee. I was directed to an area where a bunch of the guys were waiting to have their wounds taken care of. Some had been brought in on stretchers, a few with broken arms or legs. Others appeared to be suffering head injuries, as well as serious-looking abrasions to their bodies. Those were the first to be treated. It was several hours and a couple shots of morphine later before they got around to those of us with lesser injuries. Cots, more blankets, and large amounts of clothes were brought in to the area, as well as a temporary soup kitchen.

After I had eaten I felt better, but exhaustion had set in big time. I was issued a cot, a couple more blankets, skivvies, shoes, and fatigues. I spent the remainder of the day and all night sleeping.

On my second run through the chow line, I met Kurth and Pop Schuber.

"You guys look like you been through a hurricane, or a tornado, or whatever the hell they call em out here."

"You don't look too good yourself, Dude," Pop said. "They call em typhoons. I thought you would know that."

"I do know it; I just wanted to see if you knew it. Have you seen any of our guys?"

"Not yet," Kurth answered.

CHAPTER 44
AN ENIGMA

I was still agonizing over the ridiculous question the chaplain had asked. I had never been able to figure out how so many of the officers seemed to have no idea what the enlisted ranks were all about, as if we were some kind of foreign species. I often wondered if some of them didn't think all, or at least most, of us, wouldn't live through the war; that we were just expendable. What fortifies those thoughts was the way they sent wave after wave, literally thousands of us to almost certain death at the Tarawa landing.

The chaplain's question triggered my memory of an incident when we were at Kauai after the Tarawa campaign. It was during a field inspection by a two-star General. I wasn't in the ranks during the inspection as I was with First Sergeant Ruban, policing the route the General was to take on his inspection tour. I was told later however that as he passed through the ranks, looking everyone up and down, he stopped in front of my buddy, Reznik. He reached up and fastened a button Reznik had overlooked. Now that in and of itself was an unheard of act, but what was more puzzling was his comment.

He said, "What's the trouble, son, having problems at home?"

For the life of me I was never able to understand what leaving a button unfastened had to do with possibly having trouble at home, just as I was unable to understand how the chaplain's remark related to the circumstances I was in.

I was told of Reznik's answer, and I paraphrase, "No sir—no problem at home, as far as I know, except that my dad died a couple months after I left the States, after my mother died a year before that, and my sister Ellie Mae's husband was killed in the North Africa campaign. He was in the Tank Corps, under General Patton. My only problem is that I just flat out forgot to fasten that button that you just secured for me. Thank you, sir. I appreciate it."

Now I have two points I need to explain. The first is Reznik's answer to the General. Nobody, and I mean *nobody* would ever go off like that to a General, no matter how many stars he had on his shoulder and on his collar and wherever the hell else he had stars, except Reznik.

The second point is what the General said and did. It's as puzzling as what the chaplain had said to me, and the funny thing is they both said the same thing. The General knew we had recently arrived from Tarawa, and was probably trying to show some understanding for the combat we had endured there, but didn't know how, so the only thing he could come up with was, "What's the trouble, son, problems at home?"

I wonder if that question was in the "Officer's Hand Book," if such a thing existed, under the chapter, *Dealing With The Enlisted Ranks*. Sub-title, *Helpful Phrases*.

CHAPTER 45

SAYING GOODBYE

The typhoon had blown everything away, so we were issued new gear. We could now resume the waiting game for the ship that would take us home. The CBs had evidently received orders to move out as they were breaking camp and heading for the harbor to board ship. Nothing new there. Through all these campaigns they had first priority on everything, so it naturedly figured they'd be sent home before us.

I needed to get away for a while and get a handle on all the recent events. I walked to the cemetery to think things out and say goodbye to my buddies, who would not be going home. I particularly wanted to find Riley's and Hillman's gravesites and say goodbye to them. We had been together in boot camp and had served together until they got killed. I remember the second night on Betio, when I thought Hillman was dying from a head shot and asked him to die quietly so as not to draw attention to our position. It seemed like a lifetime had passed since then. I was profoundly saddened by the death of them both.

I was shocked by the number of crosses, as well as Star of David markers. I knew we had lost a lot of men there at Okinawa, but to see those many rows of crosses and realize each marker represented a dead marine, a sailor, a soldier, or an airman brought home to me the reality that these guys were there to stay. They would not be going back home to their wives, sweethearts, mothers, fathers, brothers, sisters, and friends. Their loved ones would grieve their death for many years to come, perhaps forever.

How many of the enemy had I killed, I wondered. Hell, I knew how many, right down to the man. Not the ones I *might* have killed, like in a battle where several of us were all shooting at, and killing, the same ones, but the ones I personally had killed. I knew I would never forget each and every one of those nine Jap soldiers. I've thought a lot about that.

I remembered when the Tarawa battle ended and I and others were assigned the ghastly task of dealing with the dead. There were many hundreds of bodies, and that didn't count the hundreds killed in the landing and carried out to sea by the tide or lying in the harbor weighted down by their gear. Nor did it count those completely blown to bits, "the unknown soldier," so to speak. Those we were to bury were deposited side by side in a trench, than covered with coral sand, their bodies horribly mangled and bloated. It was absolutely necessary to do it that way because of their rapid decomposition due to the extreme heat. They had been lying in one hundred twenty degrees of heat for four days and were definitely overripe. What I'll never be able to forget was the gagging, overpowering smell, and the very large blowflies. Where they came from I can't say; they just appeared. What seemed an irony was when a graveyard was established at a more convenient time and in a completely different location from where we had originally buried them. It seemed bizarre to see the grave markers in one location, knowing the bodies represented by those crosses were buried in an entirely different location. I assumed the correct number of crosses were erected, but I suppose those issues are meaningless. What isn't meaningless is the fact that those Marines will never leave that most miserable of places.

I remember thinking, as I stood in the middle of the graveyard at Okinawa those many years ago, how deeply the experiences of the war were embedded in my very being. I felt then that the memories of the war would probably overshadow and define the rest of my life. That indeed has been the case.

Back at camp I learned circumstances had taken a strange turn of events. No sooner had the CBs boarded ship, happy I'm sure at the thought of leaving Okinawa behind and heading home, when they were ordered to disembark and return to the camp they had just vacated. It seemed the typhoon had invalidated their ticket home and they were to stay and rebuild the destroyed facilities at the Yonton airfield.

I wasn't saddened by their misfortune, but was certainly overjoyed by our good fortune. We were to fill the billets they had just vacated and would be going home first. In the last analysis, it seemed a modicum of justice did exist after all. We were ordered to break camp and board ship. Unless some unforeseen disaster such as another typhoon occurred, we would soon be homeward bound.

THE END

EPILOGUE

Dennis passed away Saturday, February 21, 2004, a week after an invasive surgery his tired old body was unable to recover from. I visited him at the Kaiser hospital in Roseville, California one day before his death to try and cheer him up a bit by telling him that I had finally finished The Dennis Olson Story. Now he could read it in its completed form, I figured. I'm sorry that was not to be.

His family and the retired Marines in Grass Valley gave him his final farewell. It was a fitting and touching memorial to him, done in complete military fashion, with a twenty-one-gun salute and the final folding of his flag, that of The United States of America.

A couple weeks after the memorial, I had an opportunity to visit with Dennis' wife, Marie. She had been staying with her daughter, Vicky, and son-in-law, Chris, in their San Jose home since Dennis' death, but would be spending the weekend in her and Dennis' home a few miles outside of Nevada City. They had their own space on a hilltop in the foothills of the Sierras with a great view, surrounded by trees and all the natural beauty that area has to offer. Marie called and asked me to join her there on Sunday afternoon while Vicky and Chris were skiing at Tahoe.

Though still grieving, she seemed in quite good spirits and in due course mentioned an incident about Dennis she wanted to share with me. He had a three-inch scar on his back as well as a protrusion on his chest, she said. She had asked him many times over the years what that was all about but was never able to get an answer from him until quite recently.

His explanation was that at the conclusion of an all-night security watch and as he and others vacated their respective fox-holes, Dennis complained about his back itching and asked a buddy to see what was causing his discomfort. He was immediately led to sick bay. The itch was caused by a Japanese long-knife stuck to the hilt in his back. The corpsman extracted it, poured sulfur powder into the wound, bandaged it, and returned him to duty. Period. End of story!

The details of that incident has to be conjecture on my part because Dennis never shared it with me.

You'll recall on the night of the first day of the landing at Tarawa, Dennis became part of a detachment to protect the command post. He and Billy Joe Link shared a two-man foxhole and sometime in the wee hours were attacked by a lone Japanese soldier who rolled over Dennis, landing on his partner. With a knife in each hand, he hacked Billy Joe to death.

I believe a similar event to that is what Dennis experienced. I think it occurred at Okinawa while protecting the Yonton airfield, probably after his stay on the hospital ship. In view of the fact that he was undoubtedly sleep-deprived, it seems to me the logical conclusion to reach is that he slumped over, went to sleep, and was stabbed in the back, not unlike what had happened to Billy Joe Link at Tarawa.

I can't imagine why he felt no pain or most particularly how the blade could go through his body without penetrating a vital organ, causing him to bleed to death. Was God's hand present, or was it simply a matter of good luck? I suppose that question will forever remain unanswered.

Going to sleep on watch? An unforgivable dereliction of duty! Not something that is passed over lightly, but rather viewed as a court-martial event. Is that the reason Dennis never talked about it? While in the Navy I pulled many mid-to-four watches and can relate to fighting sleep, but a four-hour watch in a non-combat war zone can't be compared to an all-night security watch in a combat zone such as Dennis had pulled so many of on Okinawa at the Yonton airfield.

That incident adds to the already unbelievable hardships Dennis survived, in that most horrible of wars. Thousands and thousands of combatants offered up their lives, suffering as Dennis suffered, many of them dying, many more wounded. The lucky ones were those who lived through their combat and came home to their loved ones and friends. Lucky? I wonder. Did they, could they ever forget?

God bless them all for their service and for their sacrifice.

ABOUT DENNIS

I was able to secure the following account of Dennis' life prior to the war from his wife, Marie, and from his journals.

Dennis was born April 26, 1923 in Sharon, North Dakota, (Population 400). In typical fashion of the times, his mother was assisted in his birth by a midwife at a cost of five dollars.

The stock market crash of 1929 created extreme hardship to North Dakota and other plains states. His father, being an inventor of sorts supported the family by rebuilding batteries and repairing small electric motors. His main income, however, came from the Township of Sharon as Town Constable, Town Jailer, Road Commissioner, and Power Plant Operator. Each job paid a salary of fifteen dollars per month. He also served as an Elder in the Lutheran Church as well as being a member of the school board.

His mother was a hardworking homemaker active in various women's clubs.

Her parents lost their farm in Fargo to the bank through bankruptcy court, as did many farm families in those difficult depression years. They moved to Sharon and into the Olson home. That arrangement created friction, ultimately ending in the divorce of Dennis' parents, an almost unheard of event in those days. It created hardships to all concerned, most particularly to the children. The home in Sharon was sold for enough money to get the family, father excluded, to Fargo, and into a house too small for harmonious living. More friction developed, due to the lack of enough money for food, the simple necessities of life, and the privacy of all. To alleviate these problems Dennis and his older brother, Elwin, were sent back to Sharon to live with their father, an unworkable solution as he was unable to care for them properly. Like the pawns they were, their dad managed to get rid of them to his brother, their uncle, Rudy, on whose farm they were to live and work. That was in 1932. His brother Elwin was eleven years old, and Dennis was nine. Life was extremely difficult for them as they worked long and hard under the most severe weather conditions. In a backward look to those days, Dennis considers the deal between their father and their uncle to be nothing short of indentured servitude.

Dennis described North Dakota weather as six months of winter and six months of terrible weather. A typical winter day started at four a.m., when they had to leave the warmth of the bed they shared in an unheated room a few degrees above freezing. The water in the washbasin was frozen solid, making it impossible to wash, which made no difference to them as they considered washing neither necessary nor practical.

Labor in the barn started by getting the hay down from the loft to feed the livestock. He and Elwin were responsible for milking thirteen cows every morning and every evening, as well as taking care of the DeVal cream separator.

Dennis hated milking. It required balancing on a three-legged stool with his head shoved into the cow's ribs. He had to be on guard against a kick and hopefully get out of the way in time. He didn't like the smell of the cows, and didn't like being slapped across the face with a manure encrusted tail. Milking was a tiresome job that dragged on and on, cow after cow, tail after tail, teat after teat. Squeeze pull, squeeze pull. His hands got tired, his forearms got tired, and his back got tired. He hated milking. He hated the cows. He hated his uncle and everything about his stinking farm.

All farms have cats that show up at milking time. Napoleon sat calmly waiting for Dennis to squirt milk in his face. Shortly the other two, Thor and Plato, showed up for a squirt. Dennis amused himself by rationing out the milk. One squirt for the bucket, three for the cats. The cats scurried away as their enemy, the dreaded uncle Rudy, arrived on the scene.

Uncle Rudy didn't like cats, didn't like Dennis wasting milk on them, and damn sure didn't like Dennis. After a tirade of mostly Norwegian profanity, he clenched his fist and rapped Dennis on the back of his head. As he was milking the last cow she tensed, and kicked Dennis and the milk bucket, sending the bucket to the center of the filthy barn floor, and Dennis into a pile of manure. Napoleon, Thor, and Pluto appeared from out of nowhere to clean up the spilt milk, but departed when Uncle Rudy arrived to issue another refresher course in Norwegian curses and insults. Dennis picked up the milking stool, intending to smack the offensive cow, but Uncle Rudy wouldn't allow that, instead giving Dennis another knuckle wrap, pushing him out the barn door, telling him to go to school. Dennis settled for smashing the stool on a post.

In the house, his aunt Ella complained bitterly about the manure on his clothes. To teach him a lesson, she didn't let him change clothes. He was only allowed to wash his hands and face, eat breakfast, and go to school.

From farm to school was a thirty-minute walk, but for he and Elwin it took longer because they had trap lines in the ditch on both sides of the road. They got a penny each for gopher tails and a dollar each for weasel pelts. That was Dennis' lucky day. He had trapped a pure white weasel, about the length of a large banana, with a black tip on the end of its tail. It was bitterly cold that morning, but he was warmed by the knowledge that the pelt would garner a dollar, and he would be able to order the four-buckle overshoes he had seen in the MONTGOMERY WARD catalog.

The classroom was cold, but Miss Johnson had built a fire in the old potbelly stove. Dennis sat quietly at his desk, thinking how great it would be to have overshoes to keep his feet warm and dry. As the room heated up, the smell of cows and cow manure wafted through the room. No one seemed to notice, since all the kids smelled the same; however, a new, unidentifiable smell blended with the well-known smell of cow manure. That new smell couldn't be ignored. It was the weasel in Dennis' jacket pocket, which had thawed out. The smell was overpowering—similar to a dead skunk but stronger. The young teacher, unaccustomed to such a gross environment, pleaded to whoever had brought whatever it was into the classroom that was creating that ghastly smell to please, please, take it outside.

The snow bit into his face as he bucked the strong, cold, north wind on the way back to the farm. Even the prospect of new four-buckle overshoes didn't distract from his thoughts. *I hate milking. I hate the cows. I hate the farm. I hate Uncle Rudy. When I grow up I'm going to be a traveling salesman and travel as far away from North Dakota as I can.*

After the first winter, Dennis and brother Elwin had had enough. They packed what few possessions they had, basically their clothes, thanked Uncle Rudy and Aunt Ella for their hospitality, and jumped a freight train heading to Fargo, a distance of two hundred twenty-five miles. They re-united with their mother, young brother and two sisters. Their mothers parents had somehow reclaimed their farm out of foreclosure, and their mother had gotten a job. They all lived happily ever after. No, not quite.

Dennis freight-trained between his mother's house in Fargo and his father's place in Sharon, later in Minot. His education was chaotic at best. He finished first grade in Sharon, flunked second grade in Fargo, attended third grade in Sharon, fourth, fifth, and sixth grades in a country school near Fargo. He spent the next few years living with his father in Minot, completing grades seven through high school, where he graduated in June, 1942.

The war with Japan and Germany was well underway, creating opportunities of employment west of North Dakota. Dennis boarded a boxcar headed for Coeur d' Alene, Idaho, where he worked four months as a carpenter's helper. From there he went to Seattle, where he found employment at Todd Shipyard as a ship-fitter. What's a ship-fitter? He wondered.

After five months of enjoying the freedom of the big city and falling in love three times, he decided it was time to offer himself up to his country. He got off on the wrong foot at the Naval recruiting station by asking if he joined the Navy, would he have to wear that silly looking monkey suit? The Chief Petty Officer in charge, seemingly taking umbrage to his comment, escorted him to the Marine recruiting station next door, introducing him to the

Marine Sergeant in charge of recruiting. The Sergeant was glad to accommodate him. Dennis served in The United Stated Marines from March, 1943 through January, 1946.